Mynah Birds

Rosemary Low

G000270667

John Bartholomew & Son Limited
Edinburgh and London

First published in Great Britain 1976 *by*
JOHN BARTHOLOMEW & SON LIMITED
12 Duncan Street, Edinburgh EH9 1TA
And at 216 High Street, Bromley BR1 1PW

ISBN 0 7028 1002 9

1st edition

Designed and illustrated by Allard Design Group Limited
Printed in Great Britain by W. S. Cowell Limited, Ipswich, Suffolk

Contents

Acknowledgements

My thanks are due to Oliver and Boyd for permission to quote from *The Popular Handbook of Indian Birds* by Hugh Whistler.
   I should also like to thank John Fitzgibbon for providing sources of published material on the sub-species of *Gracula religiosa*.

Author's note:
Classification follows that given by J. L. Peters in *The Check-List of Birds of the World*.

Introduction

Man has long been fascinated by talking birds; history relates that in ancient Rome talking Parrots were treasured possessions housed in elaborate cages of silver, and that in India many centuries ago, Parrots were considered sacred because of their ability to mimic human speech.

It is well known, even to those with little interest in birds, that the members of the Parrot family are not the only talented mimics in the avian world. The Crow family in particular, is renowned for its ability to mimic speech and other sounds, and pet Jackdaws and Magpies, for example, may acquire a fairly extensive vocabulary. Another group of birds which are equally accomplished as mimics is that which consists of the Starlings and Grackles; from this group comes the bird considered by many to be the most talented 'talker' in the world — the Indian Hill Mynah.

As talkers, Hill Mynahs have two decided advantages over their nearest rivals, the Parrots. The first is that they do not merely repeat the words but are able to mimic to perfection the tone in which the words are spoken, leaving those who know the bird's 'family' in no possible doubt as to which member it is imitating. Probably the only Parrot capable of perfect reproduction of tone is the African Grey (*Psittacus erithacus*); Cockatoos and many other Parrots speak in a small, rather thin voice.

The other respect in which the Hill Mynah scores over the Parrot is its complete lack of self-consciousness. It is rarely that one can demonstrate the talents of a talking Parrot to strangers; they almost invariably refuse to talk in the company of those with whom they are not familiar. The Mynah, however, has no such inhibitions. It will reveal its accomplishments to anybody, even in unfamiliar surroundings.

It is this facet of its nature which makes it such a valuable proposition to owners of public houses, pet shops, etc. A good talker can be valued highly in monetary terms for it is seldom that the owner of such a bird can be persuaded to part with it. This being so, there is only one way to become the possessor of a talking Mynah — to buy a very young bird and train it.

Anyone with unlimited patience and plenty of time might become the owner of a Mynah whose fame spreads far and wide, perhaps even equalling that of a Mynah called Raffles who has been described as 'the world's most famous talking bird'. He belonged to the explorer Carveth Wells, who took him from the nest in the

African Grey Parrot

Malayan jungle. Within three months Raffles was displaying signs of an extraordinary talent for mimicry. Eventually he attracted the attention of radio producers and Hollywood film directors; Walt Disney even gave a luncheon in his honour. In 1943 Raffles earned the Lavender Heart for entertaining the wounded in hospitals across the country. Sadly, in 1947, he became ill and died at the age of eight years.

Raffles was an exceptional Mynah but there are countless others which, on a smaller scale, give pleasure not only to their owners, but to all who come in contact with them. Mynahs are intelligent birds; they are inquisitive, lively, and full of character. Young birds are easily tamed and will soon become part of the family. When speaking in their own language – which consists of a variety of whistles and chortling notes – and when mimicking human language, their cheerful demeanour makes them wonderful companions.

Where diet and cleanliness is concerned, however, they require more attention than seed-eating birds and in some ways they are more suited to life in an aviary. However, most Mynahs are kept as house pets, and careful attention must be paid to many aspects of their care if they are to remain in good condition and be a constant joy to their owners.

Deciding on a Mynah

The sight of a talented talking Mynah in a pet shop, or at a zoo or bird show, frequently induces the comment: 'I simply must have a Mynah!' It is never wise to buy a pet without careful consideration; one may be carried away by momentary enthusiasm to such an extent that the practical aspects of ownership are quite forgotten.

Let us consider some of the disadvantages of owning a Mynah as opposed to a Budgerigar, for example. First is the subject of noise. A Mynah can be irritatingly noisy; its speaking voice is much louder than that of most talking birds and its continuous whistling and mimicking can easily jar on the nerves. Like most intelligent creatures, Mynahs need plenty of company and attention so that it is unfair to delegate it to another room as soon as it becomes noisy.

These birds can also be decidedly messy in their feeding habits and are inclined to flick fruit and other foods all over the place. This means that keeping one indoors in an ordinary wire cage is out of the question as it would be impossible to keep the area surrounding the cage clean. For this reason, a box-type cage such as the metal cage sold in pet shops especially for Mynahs is essential. The latter, because of its construction, can cost twice as much as a good Budgerigar cage.

Another disadvantage is that as the Mynah feeds on fruit and other soft foods, the droppings are not firm like those of a Budgerigar, but loose and more copious. Furthermore, feeding requires a little more time and attention. The Mynah is a 'softbill' and is not as easy to cater for as a 'hardbill' (seedeater) like the Budgerigar. This does not mean that the bird's beak is soft but that it feeds mainly on soft items.

If these facts do not act as a deterrent, the prospective Mynah owner should ask himself whether he can devote enough time to the bird to prevent it becoming bored or lonely. A Mynah appreciates company as much as other intelligent pets. It will, of course, be more contented in a family where one member is at home during the day and is also more likely to become a good talker than a bird which is left alone for hours at a time.

A Mynah is not a good choice for anyone who regularly stays away from home for a few days. However, if one has to go away and cannot find a friend or neighbour to care for the bird, it is worth enquiring whether the local pet shop will care for it, as many pet shops are willing to board birds on their premises.

Those who have read about Mynahs but have never heard one talk should visit their local zoo or bird garden. Almost all such establishments have at least one talking Mynah. At London Zoo, for example, there is an aviary which contains three or four of these birds; needless to say it is one of the most popular exhibits in the zoo. It is interesting to note that Mynahs which have been kept as pets do not lose their talent for mimicry when housed in an aviary and neither will others of their kind cause them to forget the words they have been taught. The spectacle of several Mynahs talking at once, almost as though they are holding a conversation, is particularly entertaining.

A suitable cage for a Mynah, available from most pet stores

Housing a pet Mynah

Before purchasing a Hill Mynah, some thought must be given to suitable accommodation. A parrot cage, for example, is *not* suitable. The base of a parrot cage is usually square, or nearly so, and there is only one perch. A Mynah requires a cage which is much longer than it is wide so that there is room for two perches with a fair distance between them. It exercises by hopping or flying from perch to perch.

A metal cage designed especially for Hill Mynahs and obtainable from pet shops is the usual choice. These cages are attractively finished and constructed so as to prevent food being flicked out. They are enclosed on all sides with the exception of the wire front, and are very easy to keep clean. In one design a strip of metal slopes outwards from the bottom of the wire front to retain pieces of food flicked out of the front by the Mynah. There is a grill above the removable tray at the bottom of the cage.

My only criticism of this cage is its size which is usually 26¼in x 15in x 18¼in. Manufacturers have obviously attempted to keep the cost as low as possible as a larger cage, although desirable, would find fewer purchasers. In view of the small size of the cage I believe that it is essential to allow the Mynah regular exercise periods in the room – always under supervision, of course, as a Mynah can get up to a great deal of mischief. Alternatively a larger cage can be made by hand. There are a number of suitable materials, and preference should be given to those which are easily cleaned. If wood is used, all joints should be fixed with waterproof glue as this will increase the life of the cage, which will require frequent scouring. The wood should be well primed with a non-lead paint and finished with gloss paint in a light colour. Alternatively, the wood can be covered with a washable material. For a more lasting finish, the cage can be constructed from formica-covered board, the formica being used on the inside of the cage. An alternative material for the back of the cage is glass, which will have the advantage of allowing plenty of light into the cage. The glass should be removable to facilitate cleaning. If glass is used, the perch must of course be placed lengthways and not from the back of the cage to the front.

Wire cage fronts can be obtained ready-made from the larger pet shops and fanciers' suppliers. These are usually stocked in lengths up to 36in, longer fronts can be made to order by companies which produce these items, or two wire fronts can be used side by side.

Bali Mynah/Rothschilds Grackle

The front should be purchased first as the measurements of the cage (except the depth) will depend on the size of the front.

Suggested minimum measurements for a Mynah cage are 36in long and 20 to 22in wide and high. It can, of course, be larger; extra length will be appreciated by the occupant.

As a door will be included in the wire front, it is not essential to make a door in the framework of the cage, provided the door in the front is big enough to take a dish in which the Mynah can bathe. However, a large opening in the back of the cage would facilitate cleaning.

Finally, some thought must be given to the tray on the cage bottom. This should not be less than 1in in depth to allow for the use of sawdust or pet litter. The best material for the tray is metal which is hard-wearing and easy to keep clean.

Many Mynah owners prefer newspaper to sawdust as a floor covering. It is cheap and absorbent but has one drawback – some birds will tear it to shreds.

If the walls in the vicinity of a Mynah cage are not washable, they can be protected from particles of fruit and other food, by pinning sheets of cellulose, preferably the strong type used for covering books, on to the walls.

A more decorative cage for a Mynah which can be incorporated into the decor of the living room, for example in an alcove at the side of the fireplace, has a glass front with a surround of wood or Contiboard which has the effect of framing the occupant like a picture. The top of this type of cage should be made of wire netting or mesh to provide ventilation. A drop-down flap at the front of the cage below the glass panel will provide access for cleaning and feeding.

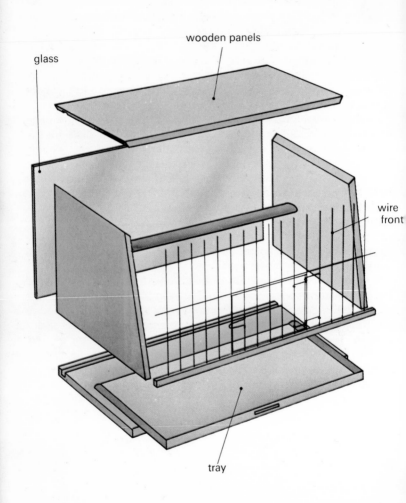

glass

wooden panels

wire front

tray

A simply-built home-made cage

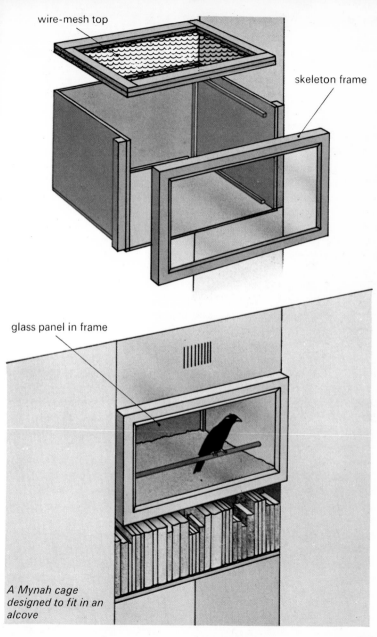

wire-mesh top

skeleton frame

glass panel in frame

A Mynah cage designed to fit in an alcove

15

Natural History of the Hill Mynah

Hill Mynahs belong to the genus (family) *Gracula* (formerly *Eulabes*) and to the species *religiosa* (also *ptilogenys*). The two sub-species, or races, generally considered to make the best talkers, are the Greater Indian Hill Mynah, also known as the Indian Grackle (*Gracula religiosa intermedia*) and the Javan Hill Mynah (*Gracula religiosa religiosa*, abbreviated as *G. r. religiosa*) which is imported in far smaller numbers.

In each sub-species the plumage is more or less alike but the size of the birds differ, as does the shape of the wattles (the yellow fleshy parts on the cheeks and nape). In young birds, however, the wattles are not properly formed, flat areas of pale yellow skin indicating where they will be. This means that only an expert can identify the young of the sub-species with any certainty (if at all). The only two sub-species imported with any regularity are the Greater, *intermedia*, and the Lesser, *indica*. A prospective purchaser should be able to distinguish these two species as the Lesser is not renowned for its talking ability.

In the Greater Hill Mynah – sometimes also called the Nepal Hill Mynah – the wattles are separated only by a small area of black feathers behind the eyes and they end in a broad pendant lobe on the nape. The average length of this species is 10 to 11in. Its natural habitat includes Burma, Thailand, Nepal, Assam, northern India, and the Himalayas. According to Hugh Whistler, it inhabits low elevations between 1,000 ft and 2,000 ft.

A very similar bird, *G. r. peninsularis*, differs only in its smaller size, and finer and shorter bill. It is found in India to the north-east of the Deccan, particularly in Orissa, and also in eastern Madhya Pradesh and northern Andhra Pradesh.

The Javan Hill Mynah is found not only in Java but in Sumatra, Borneo, South Burma, and Malaya. At 15in in length, it is one of the largest members of the genus. The wattles differ from those of *intermedia* in that the small area of bare skin below the eye is separated from the main wattle, or joined only by a very thin line. Its larger size, however, is its most obvious feature.

The Lesser Hill Mynah is found in south-west India at all altitudes up to 5,000 ft and in Ceylon at lower altitudes. It has a narrower beak than its Greater cousin, and its wattles extend from the nape to the crown in a narrow line. The patch of feathers behind and below the eye, separating the two parts of the wattle, is slightly wider than in the Greater Hill Mynah.

The other recognised sub-species, which are listed below, are restricted to islands and are not often imported; thus they are unlikely to be encountered.

G. r. andamanensis inhabits the Andaman and Nicobar islands. The wattles are joined or very narrowly separated, and the beak is longer than in *intermedia*. It has been pointed out by Addulali (*Journal of Bombay Natural History Society*, 1967, Vol. 64) that birds from Little and Great Nicobar possess 'two large naked lappets joined at the back of the neck at the top end, leaving no feathered portion in between'. This apparently distinguishes them from the other Hill Mynahs in the Andamans and the rest of the Nicobars. (If this point can be further verified, it may be used as an additional reason for the reclassification of *halibrecta*, which was originally separated because of its size.)

G. r. palawanensis is from Palawan, in the Phillipines, and nearby small islands. It measures 12 or 13in.

G. r. robusta is from the West Sumatran islands of Babi, Tuangku, Bangkaru, and Nias. At 16in long it is the largest race.

G. r. batuensis inhabits the West Sumatran islands of Tello, Siberut, Sipora, and the Pagi group. The birds of the Anambas, Tambelans, and Tioman in the South China Sea between Malaya and Borneo, are apparently indistinguishable.

G. r. venerata comes from Sumbawa in the Lesser Sunda Islands, between Bali and Timor. It is said to measure 12 to 13in.

G. r. mertensi comes from Flores, Pantar, and Alor in the same islands. It is said to be larger than *venerata*.

G. r. enganensis from Engan was originally separated but is now considered synonymous with *G. r. religiosa*.

The only Hill Mynah which lacks wattles on the *side* of the face is classified as a separate species – *Gracula ptilogenys*, the Ceylon Mynah. The long pendant lobe is present on each side of the neck, as in *religiosa*. In *Birds of Ceylon*, Vol. 11, Col. Legge stated: 'This handsome bird frequents for the most part the tops of tall trees; it associates in small parties, and is very partial to the sides of deep ravines, lofty precipices, and overhanging woods. It is fond of launching itself out into mid-air from these dizzy heights, uttering its shrill metallic-sounding whistle and loud calls, and circling round, it returns to its lofty perch on the top of some huge Doon-tree, and there continues the exercise of its vocal powers . . . The Mynah talks well, and is eagerly sought after as a caged bird,

The origins of the Mynah

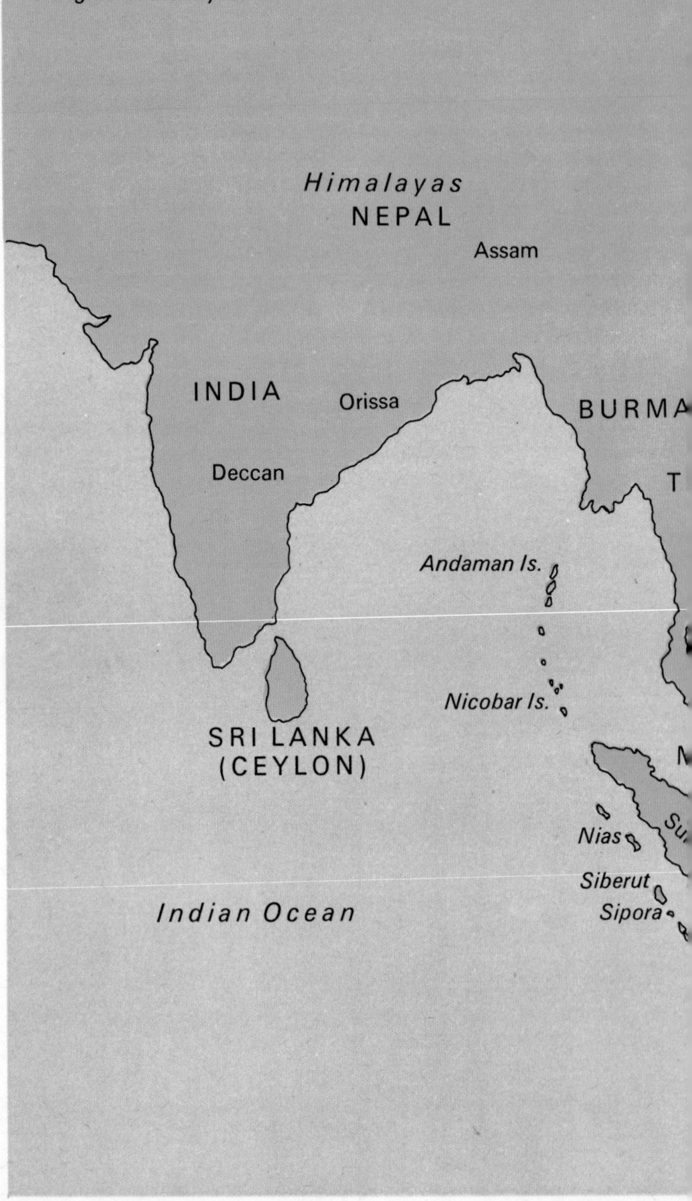
Himalayas
NEPAL
Assam
INDIA
Orissa
BURMA
Deccan
T
Andaman Is.
Nicobar Is.
SRI LANKA
(CEYLON)
Nias
Siberut
Sipora
Indian Ocean

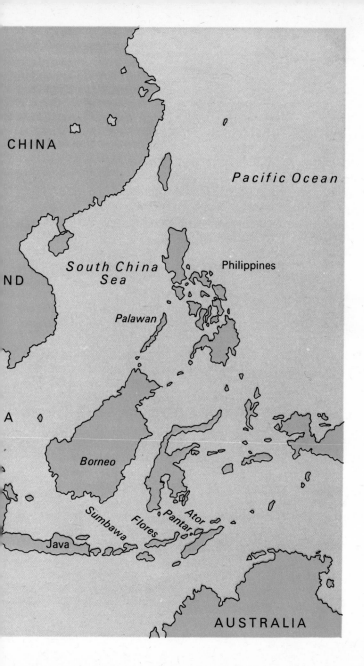

CHINA

Pacific Ocean

South China
Sea

ND

Philippines

Palawan

A

Borneo

Sumbawa

Flores

Pantar

Ator

Java

AUSTRALIA

19

and much prized by the Kandyans as a pet, as it is extremely difficult to procure from the nest.' Its feeding and nesting habits do not differ from those of the *religiosa* species.

The Hill Mynahs spend most of their lives in trees. They inhabit all kinds of forests, evergreen and deciduous alike, and are found in plantations. After the breeding season they are partially migratory, moving to areas where there is ripening fruit, especially that of the ficus trees. Flocks numbering as many as 100 birds have been seen, which rapidly clear the trees of fruit.

In *The Popular Handbook of Indian Birds* Hugh Whistler wrote: 'Out of the breeding season it is found in small parties and flocks which keep very largely to the tops of the trees unless curiosity brings them to the lower boughs to investigate some local movement or phenomenon. They do occasionally visit the ground and there they progress not by walking like other Mynahs and Starlings but by Sparrow-like hops. The flight is straight and powerful. The chief characteristic, however, is their voices; they are very noisy, using a great variety of notes, some melodious, some wheezing and some harsh shrieking . . .

'The breeding season is mainly from February to May but a few nests may be found later until October. The nest is a miscellaneous collection, sometimes very small, of grass, feathers, dirt and touchwood in the bottom of a hole in a tree from 10 to 40 feet from the ground. The tree chosen is by preference a dead one, too rotten and unsafe for a man to climb, and it is usually in open ground either in a clearing in a forest or in cultivation. The nest hole is generally in the trunk and may be excavated by the Grackle itself.

'The clutch consists of two or three eggs. In shape these are very regular ovals, the shell being very close and fine but with little gloss. The ground colour is a delicate pale sea-green or greenish-blue, more or less profusely spotted and splashed with pale purple, purplish-brown and chocolate-brown.'

Almost all the Greater Hill Mynahs exported from India are young birds which have been taken from the nest and hand-reared. Under normal circumstances this would be far from easy as these birds nest in inaccessible places. The natives of the Garo Hills District of Assam, however, have induced the local Mynahs to use artificial nests.

The young Mynahs are fed by the natives on boiled rice, sattoo, and fruit, especially banana.

Choosing a Mynah

As already mentioned, Greater Hill Mynahs are rarely offered for sale once they are able to talk, thus it is necessary to obtain a young one and train it. There is a season for very young birds, which are known as 'gapers'. They are normally imported from the end of May or the beginning of June until about September. It is necessary to obtain a young Mynah since an adult bird will not learn to talk.

As relatively few pet shops stock them, an intending purchaser should look through the appropriate magazines during June. Among the dealers' advertisements young Greater Hill Mynahs will be listed. Whenever possible, the dealer should be visited. Although he will usually be willing to dispatch birds by rail, not only is the choice of a pet very much a personal thing, but one should make sure that the condition of the stock is good before purchasing a bird. In addition, it is as well to avoid having livestock sent by rail, especially over a week-end. With 'gapers', which may require feeding every few hours, a delay *en route* could be fatal.

It is essential for a prospective purchaser to be able to distinguish a Greater Hill Mynah from a Lesser. The latter species is considerably less expensive; however, while Lessers might learn to say a few words, they will never excel at this feat, although an unscrupulous dealer might try to persuade a prospective purchaser that they are equally good mimics. The features which distinguish these two sub-species have already been described.

Many other species of Mynah and Grackle besides the Hill Mynah are imported, and again these are unlikely to be good talkers. However, they are easily distinguished because only Hill Mynahs have yellow wattles on the head. The other commonly imported species are less expensive, and certain species, the Bank, Crested, and Common Mynahs, for example, are extremely cheap. In their natural habitat – India, in most cases – they are as common as the Starling is in Britain. The last chapter contains further information on these birds.

The plumage of Hill Mynahs is entirely black except for a white patch on the wing; the beak is orange and the feet are yellowish. In young birds the plumage is dull and sooty rather than glossy and may appear rather ragged; this is no cause for concern, as the feathers that grow after the first moult at six to eight months should be perfect, giving the bird a much smarter appearance.

It is essential to obtain a young bird, as older birds are unlikely to learn to talk. Young birds can usually be easily distinguished by

Hill Mynah

their behaviour. Physical differences include the flat patches of skin where the wattles will be, and the dark grey iris of the eye, which will be black or brown in adulthood, as well as the dull, sooty plumage mentioned above.

Greater Hill Mynah fledglings are usually taken from their nest holes two weeks before they can fly, and are then reared by hand, which explains why young imported birds are so tame and gape for food. Lesser Hill Mynahs, on the other hand, are often captured as adults which is probably why they do not become good mimics.

The other essential point is to obtain a healthy bird. As feather condition is no indication of health in a young bird, one must look for other signs. The eyes should be looked at closely not only because a healthy bird is bright-eyed and alert, but also because eye infections in young Mynahs are not uncommon. There are two reasons for this: young birds kept together tend to peck playfully at

22

each other's eyes, and Mynahs also have a tendency to rub their faces on the perches which may be soiled.

The feet should also be inspected to make sure that they are perfect, although a missing nail is of little consequence unless one intends to exhibit the bird.

It is extremely difficult to pick out a particular Mynah from a cage-full. One that takes the eye is almost impossible to locate after all the other birds have been disturbed in an attempt to catch it, unless it has some distinguishing feature. The best method of selecting one is to ask the dealer to take out several birds and place them one·by one in a small cage, each on its own. They can then be examined at leisure. It is most important not to hurry over a decision. Remember that the chosen bird could be your companion for as long as twenty years, possibly even longer.

Caring for a Gaper and general care

The care of your young Mynah starts from the time you purchase it. You should enquire how the bird has been fed and obtain some of the same food. Some dealers mash up tinned dog meat, for example, and mix it with Mynah food from a packet, while others use puppy meal or dog biscuit with water, and may or may not mix Mynah food with it. You should also enquire if the bird is used to being hand-fed. If your bird was a present and you have no idea how it was fed previously, there is no need to worry. Mynahs are truly omnivorous and will eat almost any item of soft food put in front of them.

If you have not yet obtained a cage the Mynah can be kept temporarily in a large cardboard box with plenty of air holes. Do not dispose of this box; if your Mynah has to travel with you at any time it may be more convenient for it to travel in the box than in its cage.

The cage should be prepared with food and water and whichever type of floor covering you have decided to use before the Mynah is put into it. If the Mynah was kept first in a cardboard box with an opening smaller than the door of the cage, the Mynah can be transferred to the cage without being handled; first open the box but quickly cover it with a piece of cardboard, place this against the door of the cage, then remove the card and the Mynah will hop out. Should it be necessary to lift the Mynah from the box, hold him by placing both hands firmly around the wings and body.

After introducing the Mynah to the cage, leave him on his own for a while to get used to his new surroundings; half an hour or so later he will appreciate a feed if he is still gaping and is used to being hand-fed. Newly imported baby birds are fed by hand but they soon learn to feed themselves; if your Mynah has been on the dealer's premises for several weeks he is probably quite capable of feeding himself although he may gape for food. Offer the meal from outside the cage so that he can take it from you through the bars; placing your hand inside could upset him at first although he will soon become used to it. You will be amazed at the amount 'gapers' can eat, and at the size of pieces swallowed. Because they have such large appetites, these birds must have plenty of food at all times.

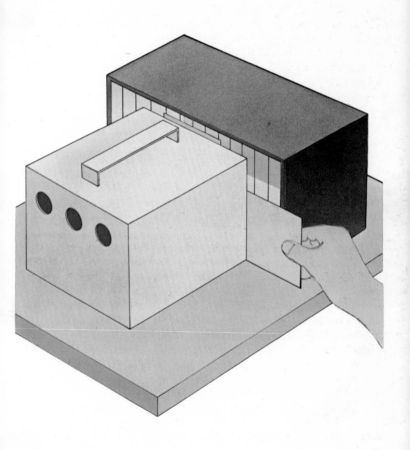

Holding the travel box next to the cage opening and using a slide eliminates the danger of escape

The correct way to hold a Gaper

Mynahs drink a great deal of water; a fact which is especially noticeable to anyone used to keeping Parrots and other seed-eating birds which drink very little. Most Mynah cages have two containers, one of which is intended for water; however, one container will not hold enough food for a day, and as Mynahs will bathe away their drinking water almost as fast as it is supplied, it is suggested that both containers are used for food. Water for drinking is best provided in a water bottle of the type used for small animals. This consists of a plastic bottle with a small metal tube attached to the bottom. A red 'ball-point' valve at the end of the tube prevents the water escaping until the Mynah pushes it up. Mynahs are attracted by the red ball and learn to drink from such bottles almost instantly. With this type of container the bird is unable to bathe the water away; thus the water lasts for three or four days and at the same time is kept clean.

Lukewarm water for bathing can be provided in a heavy dish on the floor of the cage; an enamel dog bowl is ideal as the Mynah will not be able to upset it. Like all softbills, Mynahs love to bathe and if given the opportunity will keep their plumage in immaculate condition with the lovely glossy sheen characteristic of this species.

If the bath is offered each day before the cage is cleaned out, it does not matter how wet the cage becomes. Tame birds allowed the freedom of a kitchen will even bathe in the sink – which dispenses with mopping up!

One often reads that baths should be available to pet birds only in the morning in case roosting with damp plumage results in a chill. The plumage soon dries, however, and it is quite safe to let a

Drinking fountain

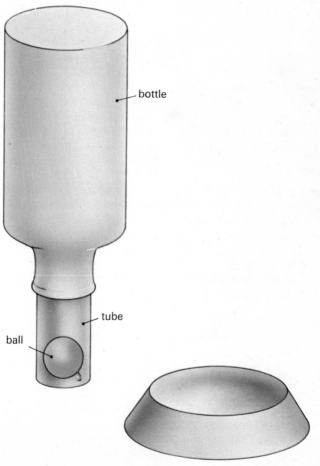

bottle

tube

ball

Bathing dish

Mynah bathe in the early evening. Wild birds such as Starlings and Blackbirds often bathe almost immediately before they roost. If it is not possible to provide a bath a Mynah should be sprayed with warm water two or three times a week.

A most important aspect of caring for a Mynah is keeping its cage clean; it will quickly become unpleasant and cause the room to smell if this task is neglected. Sheets of newspaper used as a floor covering need to be changed very frequently. The easiest way to do this is to slit a newspaper down the centre so that the top sheet can be removed as it becomes soiled; in this manner the covering may be changed six or seven times a day, though such frequent changing is unnecessary if there is a grill in the cage. In a cage with a grill, peat or pet litter makes an ideal covering for the floor but the problem with most Mynah cages is that the tray is hardly deep enough for these materials.

Great attention must be paid to the perches; ideally these should be wiped over daily with a damp cloth and thoroughly scrubbed once a week. Dirty perches are a source of eye infections as Mynahs frequently clean their beaks by wiping them on the perch on which they then rub their eyes. The back and sides of the cage must also be cleaned regularly to remove particles of fruit, and the wire grid above the tray will need daily attention. This slides out for easy cleaning. The grid prevents a Mynah from jumping on to the floor where his plumage will become soiled with droppings.

Most Mynahs will appreciate a cardboard box or paper bag placed on the floor of the cage at night; they like the privacy provided by such items and will use them for roosting, a habit which will cause much amusement to those not used to the ways of these pets. Some birds also like to rest on a flat piece of wood placed at perch level.

You should decide fairly soon after you buy your Mynah whether it will occasionally be allowed the freedom of the room. A bird which has been permanently caged for several years is likely to be bewildered if suddenly allowed out, and it would be extremely foolish to let out a newly obtained bird before it has had a chance to settle down. Chasing a bird which is not hand-tame around a room in an effort to catch it will have an adverse effect on the taming process and could well result in injury. Even a tame bird should not be let out until it is thoroughly used to its surroundings, which usually takes at least two weeks.

It is preferable not to let a Mynah out until it is tame enough to sit on its owner's hand, so taming must be carried out in the cage at first, though if your pet is *very* young and completely fearless, the following procedure will be unnecessary.

First, persuade your Mynah to feed from your hand. If it is reluctant to do so, entice it with a favourite tit-bit. A Mynah cannot bite hard like a Parrot, and so a young bird will not hurt you if he pecks at your fingers.

When he is thoroughly used to seeing your hand inside his cage, move it very slowly towards him, withdrawing it if he hops away as more harm than good will come of pursuing him. Removing one of the two main perches – if this is easily done – will make him more reluctant to retreat. Eventually he will realise that you mean no harm and will allow you to put your index finger gently beneath his front claws. Repeat this exercise until he steps on to your hand. Talk quietly to him all the time and reward him with a mealworm when he succeeds.

It is usually easier to tame a bird *outside* its cage so if hand-taming proves difficult, yet the bird is reasonably amenable, you can adopt a different approach by opening the door of the cage and placing a mealworm or tit-bit far enough outside to make it essential for him to hop out to reach it.

Whichever method is used, let your Mynah out for the first time in the evening; if it proves difficult to entice him back to his cage and he refuses to perch on your hand, the light should be turned out when he is near you; it is then a simple matter to pick him up.

Before opening the cage door all windows and doors must be closed, and cats and dogs and excitable young children removed from the room. Possible hazards such as an uncovered aquarium and deep vases should be covered and open fires protected by a guard. Never release a Mynah in a room containing furniture which forms inaccessible corners or hiding places, because the bird is sure to find its way into these. Remember, too, that droppings on carpet or furniture will stain if not removed immediately. A room containing an expensive carpet or prized corner suite is not an ideal one in which to let a Mynah fly around. Make sure that the curtains are closed because birds invariably try to fly through glass at first. However, they will soon learn that this is impossible. When your Mynah is tame enough to be held in the hand without struggling, take him near the window and put his beak against the glass to help him to realise that it is solid.

It is amusing to watch a Mynah hopping about the floor in rapid jumps – rather like an avian kangaroo. All kinds of things will be investigated by these inquisitive birds so do not leave in their way

Holding the bird and tempting with a morsel

any small items which might be mistaken for food : they could be swallowed with disastrous results.

While your Mynah has the freedom of the room 'mop up' after him immediately with absorbent paper such as kitchen towel. If he lets you carry him back to his cage or allows you to pick him up, reward him with a mealworm as soon as he is back inside ; he will then associate returning to the cage with something good.

Mynahs are playful birds and, if caged, will appreciate toys. These must be absolutely safe, however ; they must not be so small that they could be swallowed and if they are of the permanent kind, such as ping-pong balls they will need frequent cleaning. A screwed-up paper bag may provide much amusement and can be thrown away at the end of the day.

Feeding

In the wild, Hill Mynahs feed on insects, fruits, berries, and nectar. Insects taken include termites captured on the wing and larvae collected on trees. Ripe figs and the fruits of the banyan, wild cinnamon, and nutmeg are eaten; the latter are said to be swallowed whole, the mace being digested and the nut cast up. Mynahs are apparently very fond of the nectar from the flowers of trees such as *Bombax*, *Grevillia* (silver oak), *Erythrina*, coral, and silk cotton. They spend most of their time in the tree tops where they find the majority of their food; on the rare occasions when they come down to the ground, they hop like a House Sparrow rather than walk like a Starling.

Mynahs are classified as omnivorous birds, and in captivity they will accept a wide variety of foods. The basis of the diet for adult birds is a proprietary Mynah food which can be bought from pet shops; it looks very much like an ordinary insectivorous mixture but some brands require the addition of water. As a change honey and water or fruit juice can be used to moisten the food but only small quantities should be treated in this way as the food does not stay fresh so long. To this meal can be added diced fruit and table scraps like boiled or mashed potato, cooked or grated raw carrot and other cooked vegetables.

A coarse-grade proprietary softbill food is equally suitable. If preferred, one can prepare one's own, although this may not be considered worthwhile for a single bird. Fanciers with other soft-bills in their possession will find that the following mixture is avidly eaten.

The ingredients used are 4 lb of a proprietary Canary-rearing food such as Egbisco; 2 lb peanuts (shelled but not roasted); 1 lb raisins or sultanas; 2 lb cheese; 1 lb beef dripping; 1 lb soya flour; 2 lb honey; 1 lb castor sugar; 1 lb self-raising flour; six eggs – do not discard the shells; a small bottle of rose-hip syrup; and two tablespoonfuls of brewers' yeast or Phillips Yeast Mixture, obtainable from pet shops.

The eggs, sugar, and flour are mixed into a batter and the egg-shells are added after being crushed. The mixture is baked in at a low oven temperature until it is hard right through and then broken up and ground into a fine flour. The peanuts and raisins or sultanas are mixed with the grated cheese and the rearing food; the honey is heated by standing the jar in hot water and added with the rose-hip syrup to the dry ingredients. The mixture is then broken up

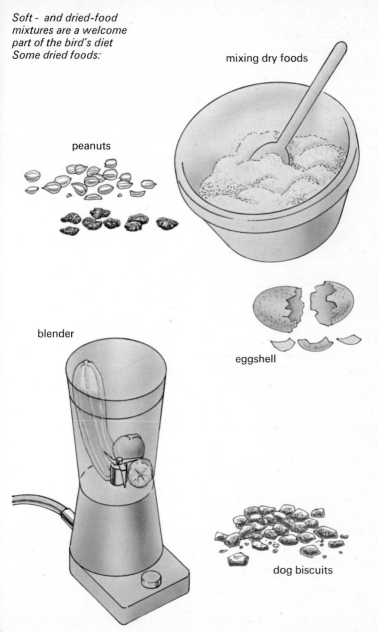

Soft - and dried-food mixtures are a welcome part of the bird's diet Some dried foods:

mixing dry foods

peanuts

blender

eggshell

dog biscuits

33

finely and can be stored for long periods in an airtight container.

As buying Mynah food in small quantities is expensive, fanciers who keep other birds will find that its cost can be halved by ordering it in 7 lb bags together with seed and other foods in quantity from large seed companies; the minimum total order is often 28 lb.

An entirely different method of making Mynah food is to put various fruits, especially banana, through a blender, reducing them to liquid which is added to a dog meal that does not contain a large amount of oil.

The use of Mynah food in pellet form has been tried in the USA but was not found to be suitable; all non-domesticated birds much prefer to pick over their food and select the various items.

Whatever type of prepared food is used, it must be considered only as the basic diet and must be supplemented with other items, especially soft fruits such as banana, grape, soft apple, ripe pear, peach, and wild berries like elder and hawthorn. Cherries and plums should have the stones removed; grapes should be halved, and other fruits cut into very small pieces. If a large slice is offered, a Mynah will either attempt to swallow it whole, causing it to be regurgitated, or it will flick pieces everywhere in an attempt to reduce it to a manageable size. If the bird is fed in the morning and left alone until the evening, the fruit can be lightly coated with a fine dog meal; this will help to keep it fresh for a longer period.

There are numerous other foods which can be offered to Mynahs, the most valuable being those which contain protein, like chopped hard-boiled egg, raw meat either in small pieces or shredded, and cereal with milk and sugar. Other items enjoyed are trifle sponge soaked in a little honey and water, boiled rice with milk and sugar, and, as already mentioned, table scraps such as cooked vegetables. Provided that common sense is used, Mynahs can be fed with almost any nutritious soft items. A Mynah will leave its owner in no doubt as to which foods are preferred and may refuse even to sample some.

Details are later given of the many kinds of insects eaten by Mynahs; when they are breeding livefood is essential as the chicks are fed principally on insects. For a pet bird livefood is not essential but Mynahs, like all softbills, relish mealworms; three or four daily will help to keep them in good condition. Only the larger pet shops stock these insects; names of other suppliers can be found in the advertisement columns of the appropriate magazines.

It is important to remember that the consistency of a Mynah's

A selection of soft-fruits suitable for your bird

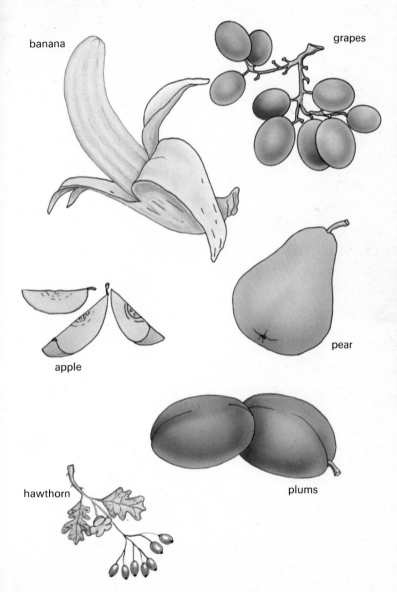

banana

grapes

apple

pear

hawthorn

plums

droppings depends to a great extent upon its food; the more fruit and other soft items provided, the looser the droppings will be, and it is unfair to the bird to withhold such foods to avoid the inconveniences caused by these droppings. Anyone not prepared to put up with this feature of the Mynah is advised to buy a Budgerigar or Cockatiel; both species are good 'talkers' but, of course, neither can compare with a Hill Mynah.

Finally, it should be mentioned for the benefit of those who have not previously kept a pet bird that its care differs from that of other pets in that birds do not have set meal times but must have food in front of them at all times; a Mynah digests quickly and therefore needs to eat little and *very* often.

Cleanliness of food containers is of great importance; due to the nature of the bird's diet these will become most unpleasant if not cleaned thoroughly every day. A duplicate set of pots, which can be obtained from most pet shops or from manufacturers of Mynah cages, will prove very useful.

Teaching to talk

Teaching a Mynah to talk is a most rewarding task. These birds are natural mimics and a Hill Mynah trained when young has no equal throughout the whole of the avian kingdom, though he will cease to learn some time in his second year.

Talking Mynahs are valued highly by their owners and are very seldom offered for sale. In 1951, a New York pet shop put a figure of $5,000 on a two-year-old Greater Hill Mynah called Jerry which had a vocabulary of 150 words, and a talking Mynah can be expected to fetch *at least* two or three times the price of a gaper, and much more if its vocabulary is large.

So how does one set about training a bird to talk? The most important fact to remember is that this is a very gradual process, the Mynah extending its range phrase by phrase. Start with a short one such as 'My name is Fred' or 'What are you doing?' and repeat this every time you pass the cage, starting a few days after the bird is obtained. Also devote one or two periods of ten minutes each day to sitting by the cage and looking at the Mynah as you repeat the words; in this way you ensure that you have his full attention.

Make no attempt to teach him while he is eating or if his attention is occupied elsewhere. Old books often recommended covering the cage while giving the Mynah its lesson but this is not necessary; modern Mynah cages are closed on three sides and on the top so there should be little distraction. The room must, of course, be quiet; it is useless to attempt to teach a bird against a background of radio or television or people talking.

Speak very clearly because a Mynah copies words to perfection – and may embarrass you if your enunciation is faulty! The length of time taken by a Mynah to repeat its first phrase varies according to the ability of the bird and the amount of time devoted to teaching it – a Mynah whose owner is at home all day is likely to learn quicker. A young Mynah with an aptitude for mimicry could take only three weeks to learn its first phrase but many birds require considerably longer. Mynahs, like all birds – and especially intelligent ones – are individuals and no two react in exactly the same way. Unlike Budgerigars, in which cocks are almost invariably better mimics than hens, male and female Mynahs learn to talk equally well. This is fortunate as there is no way of sexing. Young birds and adults can be sexed with certainty only if they have laid or fertilised eggs! Every young Mynah therefore has an equal chance of becoming a talented mimic.

While a Mynah is learning its first phrase it may make all kinds of unintelligible noises which suddenly crystallise into the desired sound. When the phrase is repeated to the bird it will often react by making a typical Mynah-like chortle and will put its head on one side, thus indicating that it is listening and absorbing its lesson.

No attempt should be made to teach a second phrase until the first has been mastered to perfection. Only one person should teach a particular phrase because Mynahs can mimic tone perfectly and will therefore repeat the phrase in the voice of the teacher.

After mastering several phrases, birds will pick up words they hear repeated frequently – whether or not these were intended for the Mynah's ears. Many have become the black sheep of the family because their vocabulary is somewhat unsavory, so watch your language when within earshot of your Mynah! At Hagenbeck Zoo in Hamburg, a Hill Mynah called Agila was a source of embarrassment to the staff, not because of its fluent repetition of words in German, French, and English but because it occasionally called visitors' names. *Schweinenbande* (bunch of pigs) was its favourite description of the people who went to see it!

A Mynah's ability to talk can have more practical aspects than originally envisaged. In England a Mynah called Darkie escaped from his cage and flew into a tree in the garden. All attempts to coax him down were made in vain and ten hours later he was still sitting in the tree repeating nursery rhymes in a cheerful voice. His owner was advised that the best way to retrieve him was to play a recording of a Mynah talking. A neighbour took his tape recorder into the garden, recorded Darkie's voice and played it back at full volume. The Mynah flew down to investigate and was quickly picked up by his owner. Anyone whose Mynah escapes should bear this method in mind; attempt to entice the bird rather than chase it or climb trees in pursuit, as this is likely to lead to the Mynah taking wing and flying well out of view.

Talking birds learn to associate words with certain actions or sounds. One for example, invariably says 'Hello' when the telephone rings and 'Bye bye' when anyone puts his coat on. This word association can be put to good use: for example, every time the bird's drinker is refilled one should say 'Water, please.' The Mynah can thus remind you should you forget to give him water. Greet your pet first thing each day with 'Good morning', repeating this phrase at no other time, and you will eventually be rewarded with a cheery greeting every morning. When offering your Mynah a tit-bit say 'Thank you'. He will soon learn to repeat this.

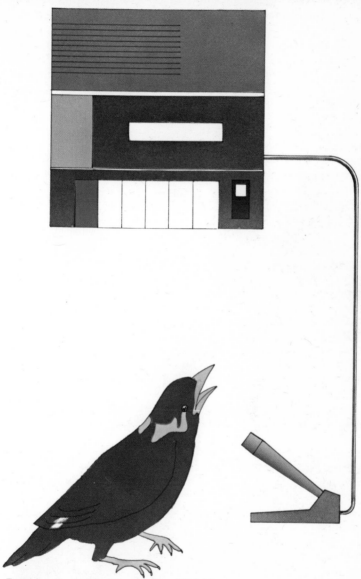

Teaching the bird to talk with the aid of a tape recorder

On many occasions a famous Mynah called Inky won the award for the best talking bird at the National Exhibition of Cage Birds, held in London. Like many Mynahs, it had a remarkable memory. Inky's owner, Mrs O'Brien, had a tame Sparrow called Sweetie Pie. Her daughter liked to feed the Sparrow and Mrs O'Brien would place its cage on the table with the reminder 'Feed Sweetie Pie'. Years after Mrs O'Brien's daughter married and left home, the Mynah would repeat this instruction whenever the Sparrow was placed on the table. One of Inky's favourite sayings was 'So what?', rendered in a tone of great sarcasm. After winning the talking bird award at the National Exhibition, he was interviewed by the actress Anne Heyward, in front of the television cameras. The Mynah's instant reply to the actress's: 'Inky, you have won again!' was 'So what?'

A Mynah at one show could almost be accused of influencing the judges when it demanded 'Where's my rosette?' Much to the delight of its owner, a junior exhibitor, it *was* awarded one.

A talking Mynah creates confusion as well as amusement. Numerous Mynahs have learned to call dogs by name, much to the consternation of the animals concerned who never learn that they are being called by a bird!

Many Mynah owners enquire about the possibility of teaching their birds to talk with the aid of a tape recorder. This can be done but results are not likely to be as satisfactory as those obtained by the normal teaching method; more attention is paid by a Mynah to its owner than to a machine. It is worth attempting this method, however, if time is at a premium, but it should be combined with some personal teaching.

In the USA a training record was made for Mynahs with specially chosen double-syllable words, which these birds seem to pick up more easily. Also in the United States – in Florida – a training school was established; however half the fun of owning a Mynah is lost if it is taught to talk by somebody else.

Mynahs are quick to imitate the sounds around them and may learn to mimic a dog barking, a door creaking, or even a baby crying. Favourite sounds are laughter and, of course, the smoker's cough. H. A. Fooks, a well-known aviculturist who kept Mynahs and many other birds in India wrote (*Foreign Birds*, Vol. 28, No. 3): 'The quickest sound my birds learnt was always my "lung-cancer" smoker's cough. One and all learnt this very quickly, and repeated it unceasingly till the verandah sounded like a chronic smoker's ward.'

Whistling comes naturally to these birds and, if taught a sequence at a time, they can learn to whistle complete tunes. This can be rather irritating, however, as they whistle so loudly. Almost all Mynahs are taught to wolf-whistle and this comes easily to them. It has been suggested that they should not be taught to whistle until they have learned several phrases as they prefer whistling to repeating words.

Breeding Hill Mynahs

Hill Mynahs are seldom bred except in zoos and bird gardens, and there are two main reasons for this: firstly there is the difficulty of obtaining a true pair since it is impossible to distinguish the sexes, and secondly there is the problem encountered in breeding all large softbills – that of providing an adequate supply of livefood.

In Britain, the first recorded breeding of the Greater Hill Mynah took place at Keston Foreign Bird Farm in 1957. The male, called Joe, was imported in 1955 and the female, Jo-Jo, was obtained the following year. In 1956 they nested twice but on each occasion the faintly speckled, bright-blue eggs were broken. Edward Boosey, proprietor of the bird farm, thought that this might have been due to the fact that no coconut husk had been fixed in the bottom of the nest-box. This was remedied in 1957, when the pair bred successfully.

The nesting material used consisted of numerous twigs and coarse grass stalks. Boosey recorded that 'when nesting, they have a curious habit of periodically carrying quite large stones into the nest-box, and these had to be removed from time to time'.

Unfortunately, the report of this breeding gives no information regarding incubation, rearing foods, or other problems, although it was recorded that on fledging the youngster differed from the hen in being smaller and lacking the high gloss on the plumage. The legs were pale whitish-yellow, as were the rudimentary wattles which consisted of small, flat patches of bare skin.

Two years later, in early 1959, another English aviculturist, E. A. Langridge, was successful in breeding the Greater Hill Mynah. His pair was provided with a Parakeet nest-box with the front broken away, leaving an entrance 9in x 4in. The box, 11in square and 18in high, was half-filled with rotted wood.

Eggs were laid in the spring and incubated by both birds, but they proved to be infertile. In July the birds nested again, using a Parakeet nest-box with a 4in-square entrance hole and a layer of sawdust 4in deep inside. The cock was seen pulling up rye grass from the aviary floor, so a large quantity of willow twigs was placed in the aviary, emulating the natural environment. The Mynahs carried some of these into the box and put grass on top.

Two eggs were laid; it was thought that these hatched about 14 August as two shells, blue with brown spots, were found in the shelter, having been carried there by the adult birds. The youngsters fledged on 16 September.

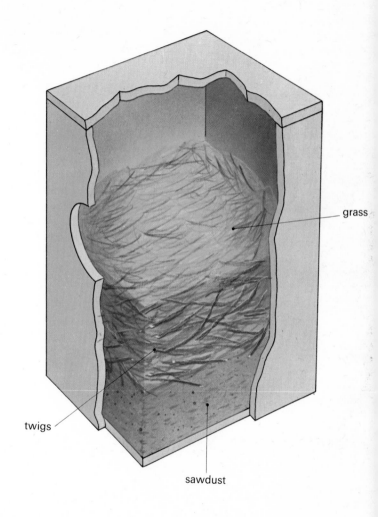

grass

twigs

sawdust

Cross-section of a nest box

There is little doubt that without the immense amount of livefood offered to these birds, especially gentles (maggots), but also spiders, grasshoppers, flies, and pupae, the chicks would not have been reared. Moths, butterflies, and wood lice were refused. In addition to the livefood, the birds ate softbill mixture, bread and milk, and cut-up grapes. White bread was used for the milk sop, brown bread being refused.

Mr Langridge noted that the hen of his pair was much larger than the cock, size being the only distinguishing feature. Boosey, on the other hand, believed that Hill Mynahs could be sexed in the same way as most Cockatoos, in that the iris of the cock's eye was black and that of the hen brown. This may have been so in his pair but the eye colour of individuals varies without any relation to their sex.

It is worth noting the words of V. R. Lilley, who had five Greater Hill Mynahs in his care at Waddesdon Manor in England, two of which successfully reared young. He wrote (*Cage and Aviary Birds*, 7 January 1971): 'All five Mynahs have been very carefully examined in an attempt to discover a means of sexing them, and I am prepared to state that there is no reliable method. Any claims to the contrary by so-called experts should be regarded with the utmost suspicion.'

All kinds of theories have been put forward regarding sexing Mynahs but Mr Lilley is probably right in thinking that there is no reliable method. It has been stated that the male is bolder in appearance and larger, with longer wattles on the nape of the neck. The pelvic bone test has also been suggested, in which those birds in which the pelvic bones are wider apart, to allow egg-laying, are classified as females. However, in immature females and those not in breeding condition, the pelvic bones could be the same distance apart as those of a male. Another theory is that the small feathered area on the side of the face, between the wattles and shaped rather like a 'V' on its side, is larger in the male.

To revert to the breeding at Waddesdon Manor, Dandy, the first bird, was acquired in 1965 and another, Giles, in 1967. Giles had been a family pet and both birds were good talkers. In 1968 two more Hill Mynahs were added to the collection, including one called Peter. The four birds were kept in an aviary measuring 21 ft x 21 ft x 20 ft high. Grass covered part of the floor and there was a water fountain in the centre. Pennant's Parakeets, Gallinules, a Touraco, and a pair of Lavender Ice Pigeons shared the enclosure.

The bird named Giles, which was approximately $5\frac{1}{2}$ years old, always slept in the nest-box provided for the Pennant's Parakeets;

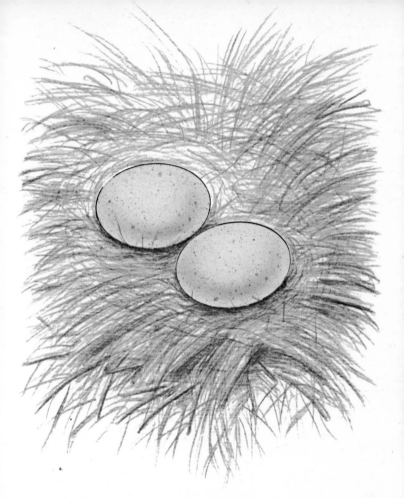

Mynah birds' eggs are blue-green spotted with brown; they are large in comparison with the average size of a Mynah

this measured 10in square and 2 ft deep with a 3in entrance hole. It was placed in the flight area approximately 9 ft from the ground.

The Mynahs had never shown any interest in each other, even in June 1970, when Giles was seen to carry hay into the nest-box. When the box was inspected on 12 June one egg was inside. This was described as being '39 mm x 27 mm, pale greenish-blue with pale to mid-brown spots of irregular size and shape'. Later, a second egg was laid.

When the nest was inspected on 12 July a chick was found, so the amount of livefood was immediately increased. As the Ice Pigeons were eating most of the mealworms and other insects, they were removed from the aviary. Giles was the only bird seen to enter the nest-box and at this stage the identity of the male parent was unknown.

When the chick was ten days old it was noticed to have minor deformities of the legs, probably due to incorrect diet. On the eighteenth day it had what appeared to be a short piece of string in its beak; this was removed with some difficulty and was found to be 12 in long. The chick died on the following day – which was perhaps as well, considering its leg deformities. These are not uncommon in aviary-bred softbills and afflicted birds rarely live long.

Giles produced another clutch that year, the three eggs being laid on 13, 14, and 17 August. Two chicks hatched on 28 August and the third on 30 August though it died on the following day. Mr Lilley recorded:

'Incubation was carried out entirely by the hen and was of such scant duration throughout the day that it was a wonder the eggs did not become chilled. The period of incubation was 14 days and the chicks were pink and naked when hatched.

'For the first five days they were fed entirely by Giles, who had access to maggots, mealworms, locusts, minced beef, tinned and fresh fruit, coarse softbill food and eggfood with additional vitamins and minerals. In order to prevent the previous problems the chicks were given two milligrams of the egg rearing food, twice a day by hand, and made very satisfactory progress.'

It was discovered that the male parent was the bird called Peter, which was known to be over four years old. As in the first round, he began to feed the chicks on the sixth day. At this stage their eyes were opened, the skin on the top of the head was black and the pale cream coloured markings of the wattles were clearly defined. The body was pink and the well-developed legs and feet were also pale cream-coloured.

At the age of ten days the chicks were given five milligrams of the eggfood by hand. Giles did not in the least resent the handling of the chicks and actually sat on Mr Lilley's shoulder while he fed them with a syringe. Mr Lilley was worried at the size of some of the food items the parents had fed to their offspring, and the unsuitability on one occasion when the hen had tried to feed two pieces of plastic-covered electric cable, 1½in long, collected on a flight to the aviary kitchen. These were regurgitated by the chicks.

On 25 September one young Mynah fledged, exactly four weeks after hatching. It was described as differing from the parents only in its slightly duller plumage and paler wattles and feet. It flew well and returned to the nest-box at night for several days, afterwards roosting on top of it.

The second chick, which fledged on 27 September, unfortunately broke one of its legs soon after its first flight around the aviary. This was incorrectly set by a veterinary surgeon, resulting in the bird breaking the other leg. Both legs were set and the bird was sewn into a light jacket, designed to allow it to move the head only, yet supporting it comfortably without any weight on its legs. This bird appeared to make good progress, but a week later it died from an internal haemorrhage. The other chick thrived and was successfully reared.

The first recorded breeding of the Lesser Hill Mynah in Britain was in 1968 at the Sub-Department of Animal Behaviour, Madingley, Cambridge. Mr B. Bartram selected five birds from a number on sale in the Calcutta bird market in February 1967. These were released into an outdoor aviary 30 ft x 10 ft x 10 ft high which was screened with polythene and heated until the summer. The shelter consisted of an enclosed portion of the end of the aviary, 3 ft in length. The birds had access to this by a single entrance hole and always retreated into the shelter when the aviary was entered.

In the spring of 1968 grass, twigs, and nest-boxes were provided. The entrance holes to the nest-boxes were surrounded with bark. At the end of April two pale-blue eggs with small speckles of pale brown were seen in a hollow of twigs and grass in one of the boxes. As the Mynahs had been given leg rings of differing colours, it could be seen that the breeding pair, which had previously lived in perfect harmony with the other Mynahs, was now chasing the other pair but ignoring the unmated bird.

The slightest disturbance caused the breeding pair to leave the nest; despite this, two chicks were hatched but died when five days old. Dissection showed that the gizzards contained a tangle of coarse grass and raw carrot, which had probably caused a blockage. Both birds added more grass to the nest, and ten days later the hen laid again. Mr Bertram wrote (*Avicultural Magazine*, Vol 75, No. 5) : 'The birds incubated sporadically and amazingly little, emerging from the nest usually after spells of only five to 15 minutes, or sooner if disturbed at all. Both sexes incubated, approximately equally, although the female sat somewhat more often and

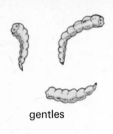

gentles

mealworms

fly

Mynahs appreciate live insect food

for longer spells. The two birds of the pair were never in the nest at the same time, except at night.'

After fourteen days the eggs hatched; the chicks were described as 'naked with whitish hairy feather strands, a yellow edge to the gape, and with eyes closed'. To prevent a recurrence of the previous misfortune, all the grass supplied as nesting material was removed from the flight, and carrot was omitted from the diet. A large amount of insect food was offered instead, particularly chopped cock-roaches, mealworms, maggots and moths: both parents fed the young. The normal diet had consisted of Sluis' Mynah food, chopped apple, pear, and carrot, hard-boiled egg, meat, and maggots.

One chick disappeared at the age of three days; the remaining one was first heard calling loudly when nine days old. At this stage pin feathers were appearing on its back; five days later black feathers had started to emerge. Mr Bertram wrote that 'the head was somewhat greenish and still bald, with smooth bare patches showing where the wattles would later grow'.

The parents fed the young bird almost entirely on insects. So ferociously did they chase the other birds that it was necessary to remove these from the aviary. On the twenty-seventh day after hatching the young Mynah fledged, never again returning to the nest. It was smaller than its parents with pale yellow wattle patches and black plumage that was sooty rather than glossy. Within two

spider

grasshopper

cockroach

days it was feeding from the food trough, although the adults fed it occasionally.

On the day after it fledged, the first of three eggs of the third clutch was laid. All hatched, but one disappeared after four days; the other two chicks were successfully reared and fledged during the middle of August. Unfortunately, the female parent died two weeks later. When the report was written, in June 1969, the young Mynah from the first nest was 'about to breed with its father'.

The breeding of Hill Mynahs is more likely to occur in zoos and bird gardens for the simple reason that these establishments usually have a number of birds, many of them given by members of the public. Pet owners almost invariably keep single birds and it seldom occurs even to aviculturists to keep pairs.

Egg-laying in pet birds kept on their own does sometimes occur. One Hill Mynah surprised its owner, after ten years in her possession, by laying two eggs during June; a few days previously it had been tearing up newspaper on the cage floor. In another instance a Lesser and Greater Hill Mynah were kept together in a cage indoors. One bird laid an egg but the other broke it almost immediately.

When a pet bird lays – be it a Mynah, Budgerigar, Parrot, or any other species – at least one egg should be left for the bird until it tires of incubating or until the egg is broken. Removing the eggs will only cause the bird to lay more.

Exhibiting

Few birds are a greater attraction at avian shows than are talking Hill Mynahs. At the National Exhibition of Cage and Aviary Birds held in London, which receives annually an entry in the region of 7,000 exhibits, one can guarantee that the most popular section with members of the general public is that where the Mynahs are displayed. This show, however, is unusual in Britain in that special classes are scheduled for talking birds. The owner of a Mynah who wishes to exhibit his pet at a local show, such as the members' show of his local cage-bird society, will usually find that there is not a class for talking birds. A Mynah must be entered in the appropriate class for large softbills in the foreign-bird section and will be judged not on its talking ability, but for the condition of its plumage.

As Mynahs are enthusiastic bathers, the plumage of a Mynah which is provided with a bath should be glossy and in good condition, and spraying the plumage in preparation for a show should not be necessary. If it is not possible to provide a bath and the Mynah is sprayed instead, then starting fourteen days before an exhibition the bird should be sprayed daily, ceasing only three days before the show, when spraying is required only if the plumage becomes soiled.

There is no point in exhibiting a Mynah in ordinary competitive classes – as opposed to talking classes – unless it is in faultless feather and has no deformities such as an overgrown beak or a missing toenail. Although it is not at all unusual for a Hill Mynah to take the award for the best foreign softbill at club shows, this would be unusual at open events where the competition is usually very much stronger.

Most foreign birds are exhibited in special show cages which are not the same as those in which the birds are normally kept. However, Hill Mynahs and Parrots can be staged in the cages in which they normally live; cages specially manufactured for Mynahs are very suitable for exhibition purposes. If a bird is normally kept in a cage which is not of very smart appearance, it would be preferable to borrow or buy a better cage rather than show the bird in poor surroundings.

Shows are held from June until December, the peak period being October and November. To exhibit with a local cage-bird society one must usually be a member. However, some societies hold open shows at which anyone can exhibit. All society members receive schedules of their society's exhibitions; to receive a

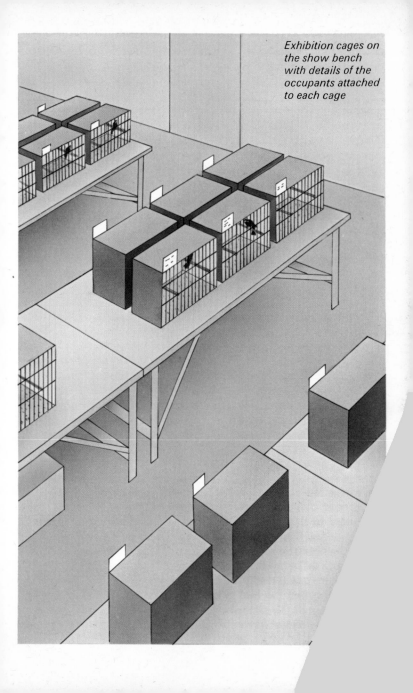

Exhibition cages on the show bench with details of the occupants attached to each cage

schedule of an open show staged by a society of which one is not a member, it is necessary to apply to the show secretary.

The entry form enclosed with the schedule must be completed and returned to the show secretary. If you are uncertain of the correct class for your Mynah, enter the words 'Hill Mynah' in the column headed 'Description' and write a brief note to the show secretary asking him to classify it.

A label bearing the class and cage number will be returned to you; this is stuck on the front of the cage at the bottom. Ensure that the cage is very clean before sending your Mynah to the show.

It is not necessary to fill the water pot since the water would be likely to spill on the journey to the show hall; on arrival, the stewards will attend to it. If you wish to provide more food than the container in the cage can hold — this will be essential for a show of longer duration than one day — place the food in a jar (a one-pound jam jar is very suitable) and label it with your Mynah's class and cage number. The stewards attending to the feeding will make sure that the food is given to the bird.

If you are exhibiting your Mynah in a talking class it is permitted to attach a list of its sayings to the cage. The judge will repeat these sayings to encourage the bird to respond.

At the National Exhibition of Cage and Aviary Birds in London, talking birds can be entered in the classes for ordinary competition and judged for condition, as well as being entered in the class for talking Mynahs. At this great show, the largest staged anywhere in the world, Mynahs more often than not win the award for the best talking bird. One reason for this is that, unlike many species, they show no inhibitions about talking in front of strangers; on the contrary, many seem to enjoy the attention they attract.

There is one point which requires careful attention when showing a Mynah during the colder months of the year. Most show halls have heating and, at least until the public is admitted, remain cool. A Mynah kept in a living room should be subjected to the lower temperature which it will encounter at a show the day before the show, and the day following its return, by being kept in an unheated room. Hill Mynahs are hardy species, a sudden pronounced drop in the temperature can give them a chill.

A Mynah transported to and from the show by car should, in cold weather, be covered with paper to prevent exposure to draughts.

*A well-lit position near the window
showing the blind for use as
protection from strong sunlight*

Warmth is beneficial in the treatment of a sick Mynah

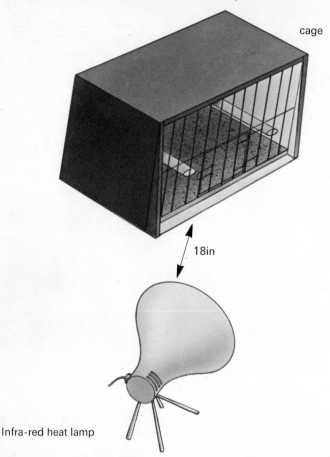

cage

18in

Infra-red heat lamp

may be helpful if the bird is suffering from shock. There is little that one can do for a bird with a broken wing except to keep it confined to its cage and to put the perch low down; only one perch should be available, to prevent the bird from attempting to fly. Broken legs can be set by an experienced veterinary surgeon who can also remove growths and tumours in some cases, depending on their nature.

Eye infections can prove difficult to cure, in particular con-junctivitis, which can be caused by a bird rubbing its head on a dirty perch, and here again the advice of a veterinarian should be sought as an antibiotic powder or cream can prove effective.

A condition which is fairly common in softbills kept in aviaries is gapes, caused by small worms which attach themselves to the bird's windpipe; the main symptoms are coughing and moving the head from side to side in an attempt to dislodge the worms. If no treatment is given, they will multiply and eventually kill the bird. The treatment for this disease is a course of Thibenzole powder, which is intended to combat worms in sheep and cattle and is available on a veterinary surgeon's prescription. Gapes is transmitted in the infected bird's droppings, which contain the worm's eggs.

Hill Mynahs as aviary birds

Provided they are properly acclimatised, Hill Mynahs are hardy enough to withstand all weathers in an unheated outdoor aviary, and are probably seen at their best in these conditions, for they are such active birds that an indoor cage greatly restricts their movements.

Hill Mynahs can either be kept in mixed company with other large softbills or two or more can be housed without any other species. An aviary used to house more than one species of softbill should be at least 20 ft long, 8 ft wide, and 7 ft high, for Mynahs and other large softbills are powerful birds, capable of inflicting serious damage or even killing each other, particularly when breeding, and in a large aviary, especially one that is planted, the birds have more opportunity to escape from the unwelcome attentions of aggressive companions. It goes without saying that Mynahs are not suitable companions for small birds, such as Finches, Waxbills, and Zosterops.

Experiences vary as to whether a breeding pair of Hill Mynahs will tolerate the company of another pair; out of the breeding season a number of birds will live together amicably but when young are hatched the situation may alter drastically. If it is intended to keep more than one pair, alternative accommodation must be available in case of trouble.

A single Mynah will be quite content in an aviary 8 ft or 10 ft long, 4 ft wide and 6 ft high. An aviary at least 14 ft long, 5 ft wide and 6 ft high is desirable for a pair, with an enclosed shelter at least 3 ft wide. It is a good idea to build the shelter with its floor 3 ft or so off the ground so that a pond can be built in the space below the shelter where the water cannot be fouled by the birds. Mynahs are excessively fond of bathing and will make good use of a pond. The sides of the pond should be sloped gently to ensure that there is no danger of a bird drowning.

The best type of wire to use for the flight area is welded mesh; 1 in square mesh is ideal for Hill Mynahs; this is stronger than wire netting and gives the aviary a neater appearance. A word of warning is necessary about joining strips of welded mesh. The makers invariably supply 'C' clips for this purpose, but these are not suitable for outdoor use as they rust very quickly. The mesh sections should therefore be threaded together with wire. To lengthen its life the mesh should be treated with a black bitumenous paint several days before the birds are introduced to the aviary.

AVIARY

Safety door

Shelter

Flight area

The mesh should extend to within a few inches of the ground; the lower part of the flight area and the aviary shelter can be built of wood but a reconstituted rock such as York stone gives a more attractive finish. It is essential that the shelter of the aviary is free from draughts and damp, and light enough to make it attractive; many birds will refuse to use a shelter which does not admit an adequate amount of light. A window is therefore necessary; this must be protected on the inside with wire netting to prevent a Mynah trying to fly through the glass window, and to prevent escape if he is successful in breaking the glass.

The bob hole or entrance to the shelter should be approximately 5in square with a landing board on each side. If it is intended to confine the occupants to the shelter at night or in bad weather, the landing board can be made in the form of a bottom-hinged door which can be bolted to close the exit.

Many Mynahs will appreciate a platform for roosting; this consists merely of a piece of board nailed just above the level of the highest perch in the shelter.

Peat is the best material for covering the floor of the shelter but sand is an acceptable substitute. In the flight area the ideal floor covering is grass, though this is not practicable in a small aviary. A concrete section under the main perch would facilitate cleaning. The entire floor can of course be made of concrete; this has the advantage of preventing rats from burrowing up from beneath, and is also easy to keep clean, especially if it slopes slightly towards a soakaway at the front of the aviary. However a hard concrete surface is not ideal for the birds' feet; moreover, any plants will have to be grown in pots. If grass is used rats can be kept out by laying wire netting over the top of the grass. Half-inch mesh is required to keep out rats; $\frac{3}{8}$in mesh would be required to keep out mice as well but this is extremely expensive.

The roof of the aviary should be constructed of wire netting as Mynahs appreciate rain on their plumage. If the aviary is in an open situation and subject to cold winds in the winter, polythene screens on timber frames can be bolted on to the sides and/or ends of the aviary in cold weather and for the winter months.

Natural perches, preferably branches from fruit, willow, or plane trees are far superior to any other form of perch; dowelling rod, for example, is too smooth and slippery, with no flexibility in it. The perches should be renewed as soon as they begin to get slippery with use and must be wiped frequently with a cloth dipped in hot soapy water.

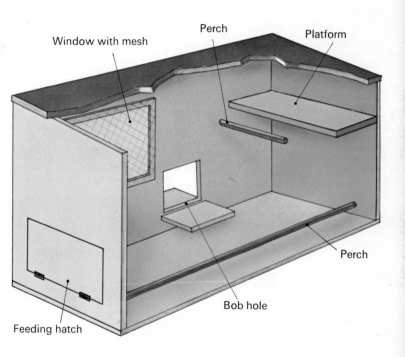

A feeding hatch placed in the side of the shelter will enable one to refill the food dishes without entering the aviary. Perches must not be situated above the feeding shelf in the shelter, or the food will become fouled with droppings. Stainless steel or earthenware dishes are ideal containers for food as they are easy to keep clean. If there is no pond, water for bathing should be given in a heavy container such as an earthenware dish and drinking water should be supplied in drinking bottles.

One or several Mynahs, particularly talking birds, will give hours of pleasure when housed in an aviary. The presence of other talking Mynahs in no way spoils a bird's ability to talk, in fact it may even stimulate the bird to mimic. Several Mynahs even create the impression that they are holding a conversation, one inadvertently giving an appropriate answer to another's enquiry of 'How are you?' or 'What's your name?'

Keeping what is hoped to be a true pair (male and female) of Mynahs outdoors is especially interesting; disappointments may be many before successful breeding is achieved but the sense of accomplishment that this will bring cannot be equalled by the mere *keeping* of any bird.

Other Mynahs for the aviary

Most of the Mynahs described in this chapter belong either to the genera *Sturnus* or to *Acridotheres*. Those of the genus *Sturnus* have been described as 'Starling-like Mynahs', in contrast to the typical Mynahs or Grackles such as the Greater Hill Mynah. All are slimmer in build than the latter species and shades of grey, brown, black, and white predominate in their plumage. Some are actually known as Starlings rather than Mynahs; others are known by both names. Both groups are natives of Asia: the African Starlings are not covered in this book.

These birds are not often kept as pets. Some individuals may learn to repeat a few words but they are not gifted enough to rival the Hill Mynahs. As aviary birds, however, they have much to recommend them, their extreme hardiness being not the least of their assets.

The *Sturnus* genus is better known to today's aviculturists than the *Acridotheres* which is imported less often than it used to be, although members of this latter genus have always been less expensive. The current price of Greater Hill Mynah babies has doubled in six or seven years. One of the reasons for this was that in 1973 restrictions were placed on the export of Indian birds, licenses being issued to selected trappers only. This had the effect of reducing the number of Hill Mynahs exported and consequently increasing their price. From the 1960s up to the time of writing, many countries throughout the world have put either a total ban or a restriction on the export of their native birds, making breeding by aviculturists of vital importance; it may be that eventually the only specimens available are aviary-bred ones.

Members of the *Sturnus* genus would be ideal subjects for domestication, as they are very willing to nest in aviaries, were it not for the vast amount of insects required to rear the youngsters. This, admittedly, is not insurmountable to the dedicated aviculturist but it is enough to deter many amateurs from attempting to build up aviary-bred strains. They may be successful with a species once or twice and then decide to concentrate on birds which are less expensive to rear.

There is one way in which the expense of providing live insects can be minimised – but it is not open to everyone. Those who live in a suitably rural area can try releasing the adult birds from the aviary soon after the chicks hatch. Provided that they are not frightened immediately after release – by a cat, for example – caus-

Parent bird entering, with food, through the hinged flap of the inner aviary

ing them to lose their bearings, the adults are not likely to stray ; the chicks will be such a strong incentive for them to return that, with luck, they will do so immediately they have collected a billful of insects.

Obviously they cannot be released by merely opening the aviary door, as this will allow cats and other predators to enter. The easiest method is to open the feeding hatch, provided that it is fairly small. Alternatively, a small flap of wire can be cut away in a prominent position, for example near a perch, but it must be possible to close the cage permanently two or three days before the young are expected to fledge, otherwise one could lose the parents and the chicks, the whole family taking off together.

Another method of reducing the cost of rearing softbills is to breed one's own livefood. Mealworms are usually recommended for this purpose but the life cycle is long. Many zoos have found African locusts to be an excellent form of livefood for the larger softbills ; it is surprising that private aviculturists have not also discovered them. The locust's life-span is approximately six weeks ; at this age it will be over 2in in length. Females should be provided with glass jars filled with sand in which to lay the several hundred eggs they produce during a period of about a month. The eggs

Breeding your own live food. Locusts can be easily bred in a large glass jar or vivarium

should be moved to an incubator which can consist simply of a glass-fronted wooden box. When they hatch, sixteen to twenty days later, the 'hoppers' are about $\frac{3}{8}$in long and should either be taken to another cage or fed at once to birds with chicks.

Locusts are easy to sex: the adult males have bright yellow heads and bodies while females are larger with fawn-coloured heads and brown bodies. They should be kept in wooden cages about 2 ft long, the front of which should be of glass or polythene. Small holes covered with perforated zinc are necessary for ventilation as the temperature must be between 27 and 30°C: one or two electric light bulbs can be used to maintain this temperature.

Three pairs of locusts can be kept in one cage, which should be furnished with twigs. Bran and grass should be provided as food.

The Mynahs described in this chapter require exactly the same care in feeding and housing as does the Hill Mynah, and two specimens of the *Sturnus* species are frequently kept in mixed collections of medium-sized softbills. Again there is only a one-in-three chance of two birds forming a true (male and female) pair, since the sexes are generally considered to be indistinguishable, and as there is no nuptial display worthy of the name their behaviour will not provide a means of determining their sex. These birds are usually rather shy nesters and incubation is sporadic, to say the least, a fact which has been commented on by almost every breeder. A classic example was that of a pair of Malabar Mynahs whose owner was unaware of the fact that the birds had eggs. They were shut in the shelter every night away from their nest – yet two chicks hatched! The nesting material must, to a certain degree, act as an insulator, but this does not entirely explain the phenomenon.

Widely varying incubation and fledging periods have been reported for the same species and even for the same pair. For instance, the young of one brood of a pair of Pagoda Mynahs fledged in thirty-five days whereas their next brood fledged at twenty-eight and twenty-nine days. The availability of livefood, which influences the growth rate, is undoubtedly one of the reasons.

The young birds are cared for by both parents, and both of them help to build the nest. Where grass is growing in the aviary, this is usually used in nest construction.

Malabar Mynah

Genus: *Sturnus*

MALABAR MYNAH or **STARLING** (*Sturnus malabaricus*)
Synonym: Grey-headed Mynah
Description: The upper parts in this species are dark silvery-grey, the feathers of the head and neck being long and pointed with whitish shafts. In the sub-species *S. m. blythii* the head is entirely white. The breast and abdomen are pinkish-brown or rufous. The feathers of the wings are blackish, edged with silvery-grey, and the tail is blackish, broadly tipped with brown. The beak is blue at the base, green in the centre, and yellow at the top, while the legs are brownish-yellow. The iris of the eye is light blue. Length: 8in.

The sexes are almost invariably described as being alike yet R. Franklin, who bred this species in 1971, recorded in *News and Views*, the magazine of the Southern Foreign Bird Club, Winter 1971 issue that 'this is not the case. The cock is a bolder bird, silver-grey on the mantle; wings, breast and lower parts a handsome chestnut brown with a white area around the vent and towards the tail which tapers to brown. On the forehead there are two white spots. The hen differs in having the chestnut colour less pronounced and lacks the white spots about the forehead.'

It would be interesting to know from other breeders whether the white spots are a consistent feature of male birds or peculiar to that particular one.

Sub-species: *S. m. blythii* from south-western India, southern Bombay to Mysore and Travancore. *S. m. malabaricus* from the Himalayan foothills in the United Provinces and Nepal south to the Central Provinces and east through Bengal and Assam to the Mishmi Hills in extreme north-east India. *S. m. assamicus* from northern and central Assam. *S. m. nemoricola* from northern Burma and north-western Yunnan south to Tenasserim; Thailand and Indo-China.

Habits in the wild: The Malabar Mynah is reputedly shy and difficult to observe and more arboreal than most Mynahs and Starlings, yet it occasionally feeds in low bushes or even on the ground. Its diet is mainly fruit, such as figs and berries, but it also takes insects and the nectar from the flowers of silk-cotton trees. This species is usually seen in flocks and small parties and its song is described as pleasant with occasional musical notes.

It nests in holes in trees, often those excavated by a Barbet or Woodpecker and which may be situated anything from 10 ft to 50 ft above the ground. The nest hole is lined with grass, rootlets, or green leaves, and three to five unmarked pale greenish-blue eggs form the clutch.

Breeding records: The Malabar Mynah has frequently been bred in captivity. The first breeder was one of the best-known aviculturists of the early years of this century – the Rev. C. D. Farrar. His pair was obtained in 1900 and laid the same year in a nest constructed of hay and lined with dry box leaves. On 15 August blue eggshells were seen on the aviary floor. For the first two days the adult birds fed the young from the crop – all food picked up was swallowed – but on 17 August they started to carry food in the bill.

Immense quantities of cockroaches and other insects were provided. The Rev. Farrar wrote (*Avicultural Magazine*, Vol. VII No. 1, November 1900): 'I watched the old birds feeding and during *fifteen minutes* they alternatively visited the nest ten times between them. They took each time *thirty* fresh wood ants' eggs *each*, or two big mealworms, or a mashed up black clock (cockroach). This went on from dawn until dusk; forty visits an hour for ten hours equals four hundred.'

Four young Malabars fledged on 2 September. In appearance they were nearly white on the head and breast, and ashy grey-brown on the back; the beaks were nearly white and the eyes were grey-blue with black pupils.

Another pair of Malabar Mynahs nested for the first time when they were at least ten years old. They were housed in an aviary which measured 25 ft x 8 ft x 7 ft high, with a 12 ft x 8 ft house attached. Their companions were a very wide variety of medium-sized softbills including Tanagers, Thrushes, Sibias, Bulbuls, Fruitsuckers, and two other members of the Sturnidae – the Pagoda Mynah and the Rosy Pastor. It is worth recording that in all their years together, these two Malabar Mynahs had never displayed any interest in each other, causing their owner to doubt that they were a true pair – although one was more brightly coloured than the other and a better mimic and whistler.

Mating, display, or carrying of nesting material was not observed at any time but when one bird was seen leaving a nest-box an inspection revealed two blue eggs. The box had been hollowed out of a poplar log and measured 16in deep, with an inside diameter of about 7in. Green leaves, small twigs, and grass had been used to line the nest.

It has already been mentioned that incubation on the part of many Mynahs is sporadic – and the same pair of Malabars was used to illustrate this point. The two chicks that hatched were both fed by the hen; the cock was never seen near the nest-box.

Another pair which successfully reared young also nested in a hollowed-out poplar log with a 4in hole through the centre. The cock was seen carrying green grass into the log. On 19 July the first chick was heard cheeping and pieces of eggshell were found in the aviary. Two chicks fledged on 28 July and while they were being reared, the normal diet of fruit, softfood, and maggots was supplemented with large quantities of flies and mealworms.

ANDAMAN MYNAH (*Sturnus erythropygius andamanensis*)
Description: The plumage is entirely black and white; the wings and tail are black, the remainder being white. The bill is yellow and the naked skin surrounding the eye is pale yellow. Length: 8in.
Sub-species: *S. e. andamanensis* from the Andaman Islands in the Bay of Bengal. *S. e. erythropygius* from Car Nicobar, Nicobar Islands. *S. e. katchalensis* from Katchal Island, Nicobars.
Remarks: A few specimens of this Mynah are imported from time to time but it is not very well known as an aviary bird.
Breeding records: Almost certainly the first breeder in Britain

was the Rev. C. D. Farrar. His pair were observed carrying straw into a log in the aviary which they shared with a pair of Turquoisine Parakeets. Incubation of the deep-blue eggs was carried out by the hen for about thirteen days; when the chicks hatched they were fed by both parents and large quantities of mealworms were consumed.

In *Through A Birdroom Window* (published about 1930) the Rev. Farrar recorded: 'On Saturday August 1st, youngster No. 1 made its appearance, fully fledged. Three others followed on Sunday, or rather, to be correct, two flew out and one popped its head out of the log; so I knew that my patience had been rewarded, and that I was the proud and happy possessor of four young Andaman Starlings. The youngsters have the black on their wings beautifully laced with white, their waistcoats are snowy white, their tails greyish, their beaks pinkish, as also their legs; their eyes are the same as their parents'. They have a grey mark down the back of the head, where their parents are white.'

Andaman Mynah

PAGODA MYNAH (*Sturnus pagodarum*)

Synonyms: Black-headed Mynah, Brahminy Minah

Description: The most conspicuous feature is the long, black crest which lays flat on the head, except in song or display. The upper parts are grey, except for the outer flight feathers which are black. The sides of the head, the neck, and the under parts are rich buff to reddish-fawn, with the exception of the white thighs and a white patch below the tail. The brown tail is broadly tipped with white. The bill is blue at the base, greenish in the centre and yellow at the tip. The legs are yellow. The sexes are alike in plumage. Immature birds are much duller, being sooty brown and without the crest. Length: 8in.

Distribution: The Pagoda Mynah is widespread throughout India, Sri Lanka (Ceylon), Nepal, and eastern Afghanistan; it is absent only from the arid regions of the north-west of India. In the Himalayas it is commonly found up to 4,000 ft and has been recorded up to 8,000 ft.

Habits in the wild: The Pagoda Mynah is usually seen in pairs, or small flocks of six to twelve individuals. It feeds on the ground and in trees where it takes figs, berries, and other fruit, and the nectar of flowers such as the silk cotton. It is also said to take grasshoppers and other insects from among the feet of grazing cattle.

Open, well-cultivated areas with plenty of trees are its favourite habitat, thus it enters gardens and is frequently seen near houses: in this respect it can be compared with our own Starling (*Sturnus vulgaris*). It is equally as catholic as that species in its choice of a nesting site which may consist of a hole in a tree or in the roof of a house or other building at least 15 ft from the ground, though nest-boxes are also used. The nesting hole is lined with feathers, dry grass, or dead leaves, and three to five unmarked pale-blue or greenish-blue eggs are laid. The bird has a song consisting of various chattering notes; while singing it nods its head and raises its crest.

Breeding records: This Mynah is easily persuaded to nest in an aviary, and provided that adequate supplies of livefood are available no difficulties should be encountered in rearing the young. One fancier who bred these birds provided her pair with a Parakeet nest-box measuring 12in x 8in when she saw the cock carrying twigs and dried grass. Two eggs were laid, although it appeared that the hen seldom visited the nest. Despite this, both eggs hatched and the chicks did well for ten days, until they were found dead on the floor, victims of interference by the other birds in the aviary –

Bulbuls, Starlings and Thrushes. The Mynahs nested again and laid two more eggs which both proved to be infertile. In a third nest, one of the two eggs hatched and the chick fledged at the age of four weeks.

The Rev. C. D. Farrar recorded his success in breeding Pagoda Mynahs in his book *Through a Birdroom Window*. His pair built a nest from small sticks and lined it with leaves from a box shrub. He recorded: 'The cock and the hen took it by turns to sit, and I think they took certain watches, and not day and night spells.' The eggs were described as 'small and blue, like those of our common Starling'. Incubation lasted approximately thirteen days.

The Rev. Farrar found that when the chicks hatched the adults were very fond of fresh ants' eggs, whereas his Andaman Mynahs, which were also rearing chicks, would hardly look at them. He found that 'the Pagoda parents were the shyest of feeders after the first week. I could never catch them at it, watch as I might. For the first week they did not mind a bit. The Andamans, on the other hand, were very shy at first, and got bolder as the days went on.'

The three young Pagodas were described as 'brown little things with Jackdaw eyes, a black spot on the crown where the crest will one day be; yellow beaks, but no blue on them, and pink feet'.

It is worth recording that on one occasion, when a pair of Pagoda Mynahs reared young in a mixed aviary, the adult birds tore to pieces chicks of Bengalese and Zebra Finches in order to feed them to their young. Insects were provided – but evidently not enough to satisfy the adults. The young Mynahs fledged at the age of thirty-five days but two had both legs deformed and had to be destroyed. One of the remaining two was killed by the parents, who harrassed it perpetually.

While the chicks in the second nest were being reared an abundant supply of smooth caterpillars, gentles, and mealworms was available, and the two chicks thrived. Fledging after twenty-eight and twenty-nine days, they were larger and more brightly coloured than the young from the first nest. At four weeks old they were larger than their fourteen-week-old brother.

The Pagoda Mynah crosses freely with other members of the genus. Aiming for such hybrids is not to be recommended, but in large, mixed aviaries one has no control over such matings other than to make sure that true pairs are housed together.

In the large Temperate Bird House at Chester Zoo a male Pagoda Mynah and a female Malabar reared two youngsters in 1966. The nesting site chosen was a hole in a circular pole supporting the roof

72

Pagoda Mynah

at a height of 9 ft. The entrance hole was so small that the Pagoda found entry difficult. Due to the site chosen, it was not possible to examine the nest but it was recorded that both parents fed the youngsters on maggots, flies, and small pieces of meat. On fledging they were described as resembling the Malabar Mynah in size and general colouration but with a dark-grey cap and almost-grey underparts.

The cross was first obtained by H. Whitley at Paignton in 1927 when one youngster was reared; four more were bred in 1928. A Scottish aviculturist crossbred again in 1969 as a result of loosing one bird of each pair. The new parents were flying in an aviary approximately 18 ft x 8 ft x 6 ft 6in high and it was not until the birds were seen carrying mealworms to the nest-box that it was known they were nesting. The chicks lived for a week only.

Four eggs were laid in the second clutch, three of which hatched and were reared, mealworms and maggots forming a large part of the diet. It is interesting to note that each youngster differed in its plumage pattern; one had a black head like the Pagoda, another had a black head with a small white patch at the front and in the third the front part of the head was white and the rear black.

In the aviaries of Edward Marshall Boehm, in New Jersey, USA, a hen Pagoda Mynah reared two youngsters when paired with a Rosy Pastor (*Sturnus roseus*) although in the aviary at the same time were potential sex partners of the same species for each bird, as well as a pair of Pagodas who hatched youngsters on the same day as the mixed pair: the hybrid youngsters fledged two days before the true Pagodas. The latter were described as miniatures of the adults but paler in colour, while the hybrids were smoky-grey on the wings and mantle with paler underparts and dark cap.

Remarks: A Pagoda Mynah, blind in one eye, lived for twelve years as a house pet. It was described as a most entertaining and knowledgeable bird and learned to say 'Hello, Boy'.

PIED MYNAH (*Sturnus contra*)

Description: The upper parts are black or brownish-black except for a prominent white patch on the side of the face, a white rump, and a white line across the wings. The upper breast is black, the rest of the underparts being vinaceous-grey to buff. The iris and the legs are yellowish-white, the eyelids and a bare patch in front of each eye being orange. The longish, pointed beak is orange at the base and whitish-yellow elsewhere. Length: 9in.

Sub-species: *S. c. contra*, a native of the plains of Nepal and northern India from United and Central Provinces to Assam. *S. c. superciliaris* from Manipur in the extreme east of India, and Burma, south to the Mergui district. *S. c. floweri* from southern Burma, Thailand and western Indo-China. *S. c. jalla* from Sumatra, Java and Bali.

Habits in the wild: This is a very common species, and is found either in small groups, or in flocks of several hundred. It feeds

Pied Mynah

mainly on the ground, often among cattle, and searches for insects such as grasshoppers, beetles, caterpillars, crickets, and ants, and will also take worms; fruit, especially that of the Ficus trees, berries, and grain are also eaten. It is principally a bird of open and cultivated country, often frequenting gardens and the vicinity of houses, but never settling on the buildings.

Its nest is said to be very different from that of other Mynahs, only very rarely being built in a hole. It is a large, untidy structure, usually globular, and constructed from twigs, straw, grass, leaves, and even rubbish such as rags, with feathers used as a lining. Nests are normally 10 ft to 30 ft above the ground and it is not unusual for there to be a number in one tree. Five eggs, less often four or six, are laid, and these are bluish-white to pale sky-blue with no markings.

Remarks: The Pied Mynah is described by Salim Ali, the Indian ornithologist, as being the most insectivorous of all the Mynahs. It is occasionally imported and those who have an opportunity to keep it in aviaries should bear this point in mind. It is also notable for its musical song and its ability to imitate the notes of other birds.

JERDON'S STARLING (*Sturnus burmannicus*)

Description: The upper parts are dark grey, the underparts purplish, and the head and breast a dirty white. The bill is tipped with red. In specimens in the wild the plumage is said to vary greatly according to the season. Length: 10in.

Sub-species: *S. b. burmannicus* from Burma, except Tenasserim. *S. b. leucocephalus* from southern Indo-China, southern and western Thailand and southern Tenasserim.

This species typically inhabits dry zones.

Breeding records: Jerdon's Starling is not as frequently imported as the Pagoda or Malabar Mynah, so there have been fewer attempts to breed it. It would appear, however, to be equally ready to nest.

In March 1970, a pair owned by R. Franklin of Chesham, Bucks, was put in an outdoor aviary 15 ft x 6 ft x 6 ft high, planted with bamboo and containing a small pond. On 24 April, two weeks after a poplar log had been hung up in the aviary, the cock was seen carrying green grass and dead leaves to it. The only display noticed was 'a peculiar bobbing of the head in the male and a spreading of the tail feathers for a few seconds followed by a gurgling sound whereat the hen would rush up to him and put her beak to his' (*Avicultural Magazine*, Vol. 78, No. 1).

On 31 May two pale-blue eggs were seen when the nest was inspected but three weeks later three smashed and partially eaten eggs were found on the floor of the flight area. The following season a larger hollow log was hung in the flight area during April but little interest was shown in it, and on 24 April two broken eggs were found on the aviary floor. During May the hen remained in the log for long periods but when the nest was inspected on 8 June there were no eggs or chicks.

A new nest-box designed for Parakeets, 30in x 9in x 9in high was therefore provided, and during the next two weeks the cock built a nest inside using green grass, a few feathers, and dead leaves. On 25 July there was one egg and on 12 July a chick was heard squeaking. The owner then supplied extra livefood, the usual maggots and mealworms being supplemented with insects caught with a large net on expeditions into the countryside, including flies and caterpillars: at no time were the parents seen feeding any softbill food to the young.

Three chicks fledged on 31 July. They were described as duller editions of the parents, with the inside of the mouth lemon yellow instead of black – a feature which assists the parents in feeding the young. One of the chicks died on the first day, another was culled because it had rickets, and the remaining youngster was removed two weeks later when the male parent became aggressive towards it. A few days later, on 18 August, two eggs were seen in the nest-box. One hatched; the chick was first heard on 29 August and was successfully reared.

Jerdon's Starling was also bred at Chester Zoo in 1973 in the large Tropical House.

MANDARIN MYNAH (*Sturnus sinensis*)

Description: The head is mainly buff-coloured with a greyish nape. The upper parts are ash-grey above, the rump and upper tail coverts creamy-buff, and the wing coverts white and creamy-buff; the remaining wing feathers are black with green or purple reflections. The tail is also black, glossed with green and buff at the tip while the breast is grey, the abdomen greyish-white, and the flanks tawny. The bill is blue, tipped with yellow.

Distribution and habits in the wild: Found in China and the islands of Formosa and Hainan, wintering in South China and as far south as Thailand and Cochin China., the Mandarin Mynah is said to seek the vicinity of human dwellings and to nest under the roofs of houses. The eggs are pale blue.

Breeding records: In 1958 a pair belonging to M. S. Henderson of Berkhamsted was housed in an aviary 12 ft long and 8 ft wide with a shelter 8 ft x 6 ft. It was planted with hollies, rhododendrons, and firs and contained a mixed collection of birds. The hen Mandarin laid three blue-green eggs in a fruit box in the shelter; these hatched on 4 July. One chick survived and left the nest on 26 July. The rearing food consisted of insectivorous mixture, maggots, and mealworms. The young Mynah was described as being brownish-grey on the breast with dark-grey wings.

The Mandarin Mynah has been known to hybridise with the Malabar Mynah. In one instance, when a male of Malabar paired with a female Mandarin, three bright-blue eggs were laid and incubated by the hen. One hatched, and the chick when fledged resembled the hen, but its wings lacked the white wing bars and its back and wings were darker than those of a true Mandarin.

Mandarin

Genus: *Leucopsar*

ROTHSCHILD'S GRACKLE or MYNAH (*Leucopsar rothschildi*)

Synonym: Bali Mynah.

Description: The most striking member of the Mynah family, it is almost entirely snowy white, only the flights and the tip of the tail being black. The erectile crest is also white and extends from the forehead to the nape, but an area of skin surrounding the eye and extending to the lores is blue. Length: 9in.

Immature birds are not pure white, being smoky-coloured on the back, and the blue skin around the eye is duller than that of the adults.

Distribution: The species inhabits the north-west coast of the island of Bali, and the island of Nusa Penida in the Lesser Sunda group.

Habits in the wild: The overpopulation of Bali, combined with an alarming growth rate, has resulted in pressure on the island's natural resources. Rothschild's Grackle is one of the species whose continued existence is endangered, partly due to its extremely limited and local distribution, so that it has been classified by the International Union for Conservation of Nature as an endangered species and it is now on the list of protected birds in Indonesia.

Among the many nature reserves on Bali are those of Bali-Barat and Sangeh, which include the natural habitat of the Rothschild's Mynah.

Remarks: Aviculturists in possession of this beautiful Mynah must maintain a sense of responsibility towards it. They have a unique opportunity to establish in captivity a species which is often very willing to nest in aviaries and whose natural habitat may not be able to maintain wild populations for many years more. With the possible exception of certain endangered Pheasants, aviculturists have never had a similar opportunity to prove their worth; it is to be hoped that they will accept the challenge which this species presents and in so doing establish it for future generations to admire.

Its care does not differ in any respect from that of the species already mentioned. It is suggested, however, that each pair or group of Rothschild's Grackles is given an aviary to itself as breeding successes are more likely without competition for livefood. This species is hardy and long-lived; a pair obtained by the renowned aviculturist Alfred Ezra before the Second World War lived until the early 1960s.

Breeding records: In an endeavour to record the location of all the Rothschild's Grackles in captivity, the Avicultural Society decided in 1968 to compile a register, and eventually a stud book. As the result of the 1968 census, 171 birds were located in 55 collections, of which 129 birds were in zoological gardens. An annual census for this species is also conducted by the *International Zoo Year Book* but this takes into account zoo birds only. The 1968 census reported that the 129 zoo birds were in 34 establishments and 29 of them had been bred in confinement. From the 1969 Avicultural Society census, it was found that of the then 178 specimens recorded, 71 were aviary-bred.

From information given by breeders who completed census forms it was found that this species resents interference when breeding and needs to feel secure within the nesting area. A densely planted aviary is thus more likely to induce it to breed.

Rothschild's Mynah, like other species, uses twigs, grasses, feathers, leaves, and other materials for the nest-box. Three or four eggs form the usual clutch, but two or five are not uncommon. As many as six clutches have been produced by one hen in one year and four nests of chicks (not all reared) by another pair.

Ejection of chicks from the nest between one and ten days is not uncommon; one pair regularly ejected the young from the nest within twenty-four hours of hatching. It was therefore decided to try to rear the young under foster parents and three pairs of Common Starlings were brought in for this purpose, but ejection of the young of both species still occurred. Eventually a hen Starling did rear two young Rothschild's, but one died just before it was due to fledge and the other about a week after. The cause was believed to be a dietary deficiency.

Established pairs often prove prolific; at Zurich Zoo a pair reared nineteen young from 1964 until the hen died in 1969. Second-generation young reared at Zurich were almost certainly the first bred in captivity, excluding birds in Indonesian zoos and some are exceedingly tame.

Breeders of this species recommend that the young are removed seven or eight days after fledging if they are independent, as there are the joint dangers that the adult birds will attack them and that they may damage the eggs of the next nest. Deaths from Rothschild's Grackles fighting among themselves and with other softbills are not uncommon – another reason why this species should not be risked in mixed company.

Probably the main hope for the survival of this Grackle lies with

Rothschilds Mynah

zoos and bird parks who can afford, more than many amateurs, the expense involved in rearing the young, although the first recorded breeding in Britain was in 1931 in the private collection of the aviculturist Alfred Ezra. The species remained rare in aviculture until the early 1960s but in 1962 a dealer in London received a consignment of thirty-five birds. A hen from this importation, bought by Mrs K. M. Scamell, reared youngsters in 1965: the previous year its companion was a hen and both birds were believed to have laid eggs. On this successful attempt, three eggs were laid, two of which hatched on 20 May. Mealworms and maggots were supplied, and also cut-up soaked figs and sultanas, dates, and shredded apple. The first chick fledged on 14 June, twenty-six days after hatching; next morning there were three young Grackles in the flight area. After fledging, they fed mainly on livefood which was gradually reduced until they were also taking softfood and fruit.

On another occasion, when mealworms were not available and the adult birds refused to feed anything but livefood, a single chick was reared on gentles which had been placed overnight in Gevral-Protein vitamin food: it was a fine specimen and fledged after twenty-six days.

Genus: *Acridotheres*

COMMON MYNAH (*Acridotheres tristis*)

Description: The head, neck, and upper breast are black; the remainder of the plumage is a rich dark brown, except for a white patch on the flight feathers and the white vent and under-tail coverts. The blackish tail is rounded and the central tail feathers are broadly tipped with white. The bill and a conspicuous area of skin below and behind the eye are bright yellow. Length: 9in.

Immature birds are duller with pale-coloured beaks and facial skin. In *A. t. melanosternus* the plumage is darker.

Sub-species: *A. t. tristis* from Afghanistan, Baluchistan, southern Russian Turkestan, India, Andaman Islands, Indo-China and Malaya. *A. t. melanosternus* from Sri Lanka (Ceylon).

The Common Mynah has been introduced into many countries, including Australia, New Zealand, and South Africa. As so often happens with introduced birds, it has successfully competed for nesting sites, ousting the native species and having a detrimental effect upon their populations.

Habits in the wild: 'The Mynah shares with the House Crow the distinction of being the commonest and best-known bird in India, being found wherever man is found, in populous city or in lonely jungle village.' So wrote Hugh Whistler in *The Popular Handbook of Indian Birds*.

Of their habits, he recorded: 'Normally these birds live in pairs and there is a very obvious affection between them. They feed together on the ground, striding along with rapid, determined paces, stopping occasionally to preen each other's feathers or to

82

Common Mynah

indulge in a few quaint remarks or gesticulations expressive of
extreme self-satisfaction. The voice is a strange mixture of harsh
gurglings and liquid notes, *keeky-keeky-keeky*, *churr-churr*, *kok-
kok-kok*, and the last notes are invariably accompanied by a quaint,
stiff bobbing of the head, generally close in front of the male.'

Before dusk, parties of Common Mynahs collect into large flocks
and sleep in grooves in trees. The noise, as they settle down for the
night, can be compared with the communal roosts of Starlings
known all over the world, and indeed, Starlings and Bank Mynahs
often roost with the Common Mynahs.

This species feeds on a wide variety of items, especially insects. In *A Guide to the Birds of Ceylon*, G. M. Henry states that the Celanese race 'is much given to attending on cattle and buffaloes, for the sake of the ticks which infest them, and the insects which are disturbed by their feet as they graze. It lives largely on grasshoppers.' The Common Mynah also eats locusts, crickets, caterpillars, grubs, and earthworms, in addition to household scraps, fruit, and grain.

The nest is found in the roofs of houses, holes in walls and trees, nest-boxes, and nests formerly occupied by kites, crows, or squirrels. Materials used in construction include straw, twigs, feathers, and rubbish of various sorts. The clutch numbers three to six eggs, more often four or five. They are pale blue or greenish-blue and unmarked.

Remarks: This is the bird most likely to be confused with the Hill Mynah. It may become quite a good mimic and learn to repeat a few words if obtained when young, but its talent for mimicry cannot be compared with that of the Hill Mynah although it is an attractive aviary bird, full of character.

One aviculturist who kept a specimen at liberty found it to be an excellent 'stayer' and a great attraction in his garden. Although it was far from tame when kept in an aviary, when allowed complete freedom it became much more docile and would almost take mealworms from its owner's hand. It had a passion for earwigs and would walk sedately along the garden path tapping the wooden stakes to which the dahlias were tied, in order to dislodge these insects.

BANK MYNAH (*Acridotheres ginginianus*)

Synonym: Indian Mynah.

Description: This species is very similar to the Common Mynah, but differs in its slatey-grey colouration and in the naked skin around the eyes which is brick-red instead of yellow. The centre of the abdomen is pinkish-buff. The legs are yellow, the beak yellow or orange, and the iris dark red. The plumage is duller in immature birds. Length: 9in.

Distribution: The northern half of India and western Bombay to Bengal, Nepal, and western Assam.

Habits in the wild: Unlike the Common Mynah, in whose company it is quite often found, the Bank Mynah usually avoids human habitations. It is very sociable in its habits, feeding and roosting in flocks and breeding in colonies. As its name implies, it is more often found in the vicinity of rivers, where it feeds along the river's edge and nests in tunnels which it digs in the soft sandy earth of river banks or cliff faces. These tunnels are about 3in in diameter and may be as long as 7 ft: the tunnels of various pairs communicate to form a network. Nesting sites are always near water and usually over running water. Feathers, roots, and grass are used to line the nest. A clutch usually consists of four or five pale or greenish-blue eggs. The eggs retain the typical Mynah colouring and are not white as in most hole-nesters.

Remarks: The Bank Mynah is available less often than in the past. One housed in a birdroom learned to imitate Canaries and other birds kept there.

Bank Mynah

JUNGLE MYNAH (*Acridotheres fuscus*)

Description: This species and the next, the Crested Mynah, are easily distinguished from other Mynahs by an erect tuft of feathers above the nostrils and by the absence of the bare areas of skin on the face, which are characteristic of the Common and Bank Mynahs. The crest of the Jungle Mynah is less prominent than that of the Crested Mynah. The top and sides of the head of the Jungle Mynah are black, the remainder of the upper parts being dark

Jungle Mynah

brown except for the wings, which are black with a white patch at the base of the outer flight feathers. The tail is rounded and tipped with white, the under parts are ashy brown, and there is a patch of white on the under tail coverts. The iris is bright yellow in birds from India and Burma and pale blue-grey in those from southern India. The bill is bluish-black and orange-yellow and the legs are pale orange. Length: 9in.

Sub-species: *A. f. mahrattensis* from western and southern India. *A. f. fuscus* from northern India and Nepal, western Assam, eastern and southern Burma, and the Malay Peninsula. *A. f. fumidus* from north-eastern Assam. *A. f. javanicus* from Java. *A. f. cinereus* from the southern peninsula of Celebes.

Habits in the wild: This species is sometimes found near houses in company with Common Mynahs, but it is more typically a bird of the forest. In its habits and gait it greatly resembles the Common Mynah, and is probably frequently mistaken for this species. It usually nests in holes in large trees at a considerable height from the ground although walls, chimneys, and the roofs of houses are also used as nest sites.

Breeding records: This Mynah has seldom been bred in captivity. One youngster was reared in Berlin Zoo as long ago as 1893. Three bluish eggs were laid, and both parents incubated the eggs for fifteen days.

CRESTED MYNAH (*Acridotheres cristatellus*)

Description: This species is immediately recognisable by an irregular crest of recurved feathers which covers the bill from the base to the centre. The plumage is black or blue-black with a silky sheen, especially on the upper parts. There is a white patch on each wing and the tail is tipped with white. The bill is pale yellow, the feet pale orange, and the iris a deep amber yellow. Length: 10½in. Young birds are described as being brown and without the crest.

Sub-species: *A. c. cristatellus* from Yunnan and Shensi in mountainous inland China to the Yangtse Valley; also in eastern Burma, and in Luzon where it is an introduced species. *A. c. formosanus* from Formosa. *A. c. brevipennis* from Hainan Island and Indo-China south to Cochin China.

The Philippine island of Luzon is the most likely source of Crested Mynahs now in aviaries as very few birds are exported from China.

Habits in the wild: This is a very common species. It breeds in holes in trees and walls and under the eaves of houses. In *Foreign*

Birds for Cage and Aviary (Part II), A. G. Butler wrote: 'The nest is a regular rubbish-heap of dry grass, straw, leaves, feathers, etc. The wing and tail feathers of pigeons, kites, crows, and magpies are largely used. In every nest examined by Rickett there was a snake's slough or part of one, and our men were once told by a native that *every* Mynah's nest was thus provided.'

Remarks: A. G. Butler obtained a Crested Mynah in 1896 from a friend who had one 'which trumpeted, whistled most melodiously and talked Hindustani'. Butler's was an amusing and affectionate bird which whistled tunefully 'and occasionally trumpeted, after which he invariably bowed in a ludicrous fashion, making the most extraordinary rasping sound with each bow; he rarely attempted to talk but sometimes said "Joey".'

Breeding records: The Formosan sub-species of the Crested Mynah was bred in 1960 by G. W. Bratley of Yorkshire. Purchased in 1957, the Mynahs were housed with various other birds; the following year, presumably when they came into breeding condition, they killed two Starlings in the aviary and destroyed a Cockatiel's nest, probably eating the eggs. They built a nest of hay, grass, and feathers, and the hen laid four eggs which were slightly darker blue than those of the Common Starling but approximately the same size. The eggs hatched after fourteen days but the chicks died when they were half-feathered. The Mynahs nested again but the second brood of chicks died at the age of two or three days. Failure to rear the young was probably due to competition for live-food from the other softbills in the aviary.

Similar results were experienced in 1959, when three clutches of four eggs were produced. That year they were moved to an aviary containing three Pheasants and a pair of Ringneck Parakeets. No livefood was provided.

In 1960 the Mynahs nested in a lovebird nest-box. On 21 July four eggs were seen in the box, a previous clutch of four having disappeared. Chicks were heard calling on 4 August so plenty of maggots were offered, and the Pheasants were removed when it was found that they were eating half of the maggots. The young Mynahs fledged on 26 and 27 August; another left the nest on 29 August but died on 2 September, and one of the remaining chicks was found dead, apparently killed, on 10 September: the survivor was removed from the aviary on the same day. It was dull brownish-black and lacked the crest, but its legs were reddish and the beak colour was the same as that of the adults.

Crested Mynah

GOLDEN-CRESTED MYNAH (*Ampeliceps coronatus*)

Description: Perhaps the most colourful and striking of the Mynahs, the Golden-crest male has a clear yellow head, face and throat, the rest of the plumage being glossy black, except for a yellow patch on the wing. There is a small area of yellow skin surrounding the eye, and the bill and legs are orange. In the female the yellow on the head is confined to the area above the eyes, except for a small area on the chin. The crest is shorter than the male's and the skin surrounding the eye is grey. Length: 8½in.

Distribution and habits in the wild: This Mynah inhabits northern Thailand, Vietnam, Laos, the Malay Peninsula and the Tenasserim district of Burma. It is not rare in the wild but nests at a considerable height from the ground and, since it is a forest bird, the nests are difficult to find. Combined with its dark colouration and exceptionally fast flight, it must be a difficult bird to locate

Breeding records: In 1964, the first recorded breeding of this very rarely-imported species occurred in the aviaries of E. M. Boehm in New Jersey, USA. One male chick was reared; the following year six were bred, three of each sex.

Probably the only occasion on which it was bred in Britain was in 1966, by the noted aviculturist W. R. Partridge. He obtained four birds in the spring of 1964. The following spring two of the birds were removed from the aviary, leaving the breeding pair of Mynahs and a pair each of Ground Doves and Cayenne Seedeaters. Towards the end of April they nested in a hollow log hung horizontally about 5 ft from the ground. Four infertile eggs were laid in the first clutch; the second was also unsuccessful. The eggs were blue-green with brown blotches which were more numerous at the thicker end.

In 1966 they nested in the same log during April, resulting in one clear and two addled eggs. Only the hen incubated the eggs. She sat much more diligently on the second clutch, and when the nest was inspected fourteen or fifteen days after incubation was estimated to have begun, one chick and three eggs were seen. The following day a second chick, pink-skinned and devoid of body fluff, had hatched; the remaining two eggs were infertile. The chicks fledged on 1 July, at the ages of twenty-five and twenty-six days, and were independent ten days later.

At twenty-two days one chick had the distinct beginning of a yellow cap. Three weeks after leaving the nest it had a broad band of yellow from the beak to a line slightly behind the eye, whereas its nest mate had only a small amount of yellow, just above the beak. There was little doubt that they were male and female.

Food provided during the rearing period included minced raw meat, maggots, apple, insects, and soaked biscuit meal. For the first few days livefood only was fed to the chicks.

Remarks: As this Mynah is so little known in aviculture, it is worth recording the observations of the authority on Indian birds, Fram Finn. He wrote: 'This bird is, in my opinion, quite wrongly placed by Oates among the typical Starlings or Mynahs. It should go among the Hill-Mynah section, which it resembles in its hopping gait on the ground, in its heavy build, and in its style of plumage; but I think there is no sufficient reason for making a family distinction between these two groups' (*Avicultural Magazine*, Vol. VII, July 1909).

Golden Crested Mynah

Index